BOOKKEEPING

Beginner's Guide to Basic Bookkeeping and Accounting Principles to Build a Successful Business

ABRAHAM DOUGLAS

© **Copyright 2019 by <u>Abraham Douglas</u>- All rights reserved.**

This document is geared towards providing exact and reliable information in regards to the topic and issue covered. The publication is sold with the idea that the publisher is not required to render accounting, officially permitted, or otherwise, qualified services. If advice is necessary, legal or professional, a practiced individual in the profession should be ordered.

- From a Declaration of Principles which was accepted and approved equally by a Committee of the American Bar Association and a Committee of Publishers and Associations.

In no way is it legal to reproduce, duplicate, or transmit any part of this document in either electronic means or in printed format. Recording of this publication is strictly prohibited and any storage of this document is not allowed unless with written permission from the publisher. All rights reserved.

The information provided herein is stated to be truthful and consistent, in that any liability, in terms of inattention or otherwise, by any usage or abuse of any policies, processes, or directions contained within is the solitary and utter responsibility of the recipient reader. Under no circumstances will any legal responsibility or blame be held against the publisher for any reparation, damages, or monetary loss due to the information herein, either directly or indirectly.

Respective authors own all copyrights not held by the publisher.

The information herein is offered for informational purposes solely, and is universal as so. The presentation of the information is without contract or any type of guarantee assurance.

The trademarks that are used are without any consent, and the publication of the trademark is without permission or backing by the trademark owner. All trademarks and brands within this book are for clarifying purposes only and are the owned by the owners themselves, not affiliated with this document.

TABLE OF CONTENTS

Introduction 1

Chapter One: The Need of Bookkeeping for Business 3

    A Few Basics of Bookkeeping 4

    Choosing between the Accounting Methods 4

    Assets, Liabilities, and Equity: Basic Understanding 5

    Introduction to Debits and Credits: 6

    Why you need a Chart of Accounts 6

    Importance of Maintaining a Paper Trail 6

    Importance of Updating Ledger 7

    Posting an Entry in Journals 7

    Computerized Bookkeeping is becoming Popular 8

    Importance of Effective Internal Controls 8

    How Bookkeeping Tools Can Manage your Daily Finances 9

    Inventory Control 9

    Maintain Record of Sales 10

    Managing Payroll 10

    Applying Tests for Accuracy 11

    Verifying Cash 11

    Checking your Balance 11

    Necessary Bookkeeping Corrections 11

    Time to Celebrate your Financial Success 12

Preparation of Financial Reports 12

Paying Taxes 13

Chapter Two: Understanding the Basics of Bookkeeping 14

Bookkeepers: Keepers of your Business Record 14

Understanding the Basic Bookkeeping Terms 15

Terms used in the Balance Sheet 15

Terminology used in the Income Statement 16

Other Common Terms 17

Stepping through the Accounting Cycle 19

Choosing between the Cash-Basis or
Accrual Accounting System 21

Cash-Basis Accounting require real-time Cash Movement 21

Method of Recording in Accrual Accounting System 23

Double-Entry Bookkeeping System 24

Account Debit Credit 25

Account Debit Credit 26

Principles of differentiating between Debits and Credits 26

**Chapter Three: How Charts of Accounts Ease doing
Financial Planning 28**

Introduction of Charts of Accounts 29

Explaining Balance Sheet Accounts 31

Treatment of Different Assets 31

Fixed/Long-Term Assets 33

Streamline Your Liabilities 36

Long-term Liabilities: 37

Allocation of Equity 38

Accounts Presented on the Income Statement 40

Keeping Record of Money you Make 40

Tracking Cost of Sales 41

Maintaining a Record of the Money you Spend 41

Establishing Chart of Accounts... 44

Chapter Four: Ledgers: Record of Business Transactions 46

Source of Information for a Business...................................... 46

How to make Entries in the Ledger 47

Methods of Posting Entries into the Ledger............................ 49

Adjustments Made to Rectify Errors in the Ledger 51

Chapter Five: Maintaining Journals.. 52

Prepare Transaction's Point of Entry....................................... 53

Movement of Cash 54

Maintain Record of Cash Inflows 54

Tracking Cash Outflows 56

Manage Sales to Manage your Profit....................................... 59

Track your Purchase to Control Cash Outflow 60

Posting Journal Information into Accounts............................. 62

Chapter Six: Know Your Sales 64

Gathering on Cash Sales 65

Finding the Estimation of Offers Receipts............................... 65

Recording Money Exchanges in the Books 66

Selling on Credit 67

Choosing Whether to Offer Store Credit 68

Recording Store Credit Exchanges in the Books 69

Demonstrating Out the Cash Register..................................... 70

Following Sales Discounts 71

Recording Sales Returns and Allowances 72

Checking Accounts Receivable.. 73

Tolerating Your Losses 74

Chapter Seven: Depreciating Assets **75**

What is Depreciation? 76
Identifying the Assets on the Basis of Depreciation 77
Methods used for Depreciation 78
Straight-Line 78
Total of-Years-Digits 79

Chapter Eight: Treatment of Interest as Income or Expenses...81

Self-Multiplying Dividends 82
Treatment of Interest Income 83

Chapter Nine: Closing Journals **84**

Preparing to Close: Checking for Accuracy and
Tallying Things Up 85
Focusing on Starting Exchange Subtleties 85
Outlining Diary Passages 86
Examining Outline Results 88
Getting Ready for Income 89
Presenting on the General Ledger 90
Looking at Computerized Journal Records 91

Chapter Ten: Adjusting the Books **92**

Modifying All the Right Areas 93
Deteriorating Resources 93
Dispensing Prepaid Costs 95
Tallying Stock 96
Testing Out an Adjusted Trial Balance 97
Changing Your Chart of Accounts 98

Moving Past the Catchall Miscellaneous Expenses Account 99

Chapter Eleven: Understanding the Concept of a Balance Sheet 101

What Is a Balance Sheet? 101
Partitioning and Posting your Advantages 102
Current Resources 102
Long Haul Resources 103
Recognizing your Obligations 105
Taking Help from the Balance Sheet 106
Testing your Money 107
Current Proportion 107
Basic Analysis (brisk) Proportion 107
Surveying your Obligation 108
Creating Balance Sheets Electronically 108

Chapter Twelve: Making an Income Statement 109

What Is an Income Statement? 110
Organizing the Income Statement 111
Setting up the Income Statement 112
Discovering Net Sales 112
Discovering Cost of Goods Sold 112
Drawing remaining Sums from your Worksheet 113
Measuring your Cost of Goods Sold 113
Unraveling Gross Profit 114
Checking Expenses 115
Utilizing the Income Statement to Make Business Decisions ... 116
Testing Profits 116
Profit for Sales 116

Profit for Assets 117
Profit for Equity 118
Fanning Out with Income Statement Data 118

Chapter Thirteen: Preparing Books for a New Cycle 121
Settling the General Ledger 122
Focusing on Income Statement Accounts 122
Continuing Balance Sheet Accounts 123
Directing Special Year-End Bookkeeping Tasks 123
Checking Client Accounts 124
Surveying Merchant Accounts 124
Erasing Accounts 125
Beginning the Cycle Anew 125

Chapter Fourteen: How to Manage your Cash with Books 128
Graphing the Way 128
Adjusting Your Entries 129
Posting Your Transactions 129
Following Customer Collections 129
Taking Care of Tabs Accurately and On Time 130
Arranging Profits 130
Contrasting Budget with Actual Expenses 131
Contrasting Sales Goals with Actual Sales 131
Following Cost Trends 131
Settling on Pricing Decisions 132

Conclusion 133

Introduction

Bookkeepers are the individuals who maintain and record all the financial transactions of the business. This process is known as Bookkeeping. If you agree with the concept that information is power, then you will definitely believe that bookkeepers have a tremendous amount of power in any organization. The purpose of recording financial information in the books is to help the business owners to plan, in their decision-making and to choose the future goals of the entity. With the help of appropriate financial information, you can easily forecast future sales, can make a budget, make a cost-effective decision, and ascertain the future direction of the company.

A company can only keep track of financial transactions with the help of Bookkeepers. Otherwise, a business can face various complications like fraud, misuse of funds, inappropriate decision-making, and many more wrongful actions. Without proper bookkeeping, business owners wouldn't know how many sales the business is making, how much cash is collected, and how much cash is disbursed to the employees and to the creditors during the year.

Complete and accurate Bookkeeping is beneficial for business owners as well as to those people associated with your business like financial institutions, investors, and employees. Inside, people like owners, directors, managers, and employees, as well as outside people like investors, financial institutions, and government agencies all rely on the financial information provided by the business entity.

Bookkeeping is an important job in any business organization, and that is why it requires special skills and talents. Bookkeepers must possess certain skills like vigilance, detailed orientation, and the love of performing calculations and, most importantly, the ability to be truthful and sincere when recording any financial transaction. They must maintain a proper record of all the papers and documents on which financial information is based.

Whether you are an employee of any business entity or an owner recording financial transactions of your own business, bookkeeping is crucial for the smooth running of the business operations.

Chapter One

The Need of Bookkeeping for Business

You will learn:

The Basics of Bookkeeping

How to Manage Accounts

Why Bookkeeping is Important

Definition of Bookkeeping

In this chapter, you will learn about the importance of bookkeeping, how it works, and about setting up new company books. You will also get an understanding of the unique terms used in bookkeeping and learn how to set up the roadmap for your books, the Chart of Accounts.

Due to a lack of skills and expertise, a few small business owners hire accountants to work for them full-time. For small-scale business entities, this expense is too high, so to overcome this issue, business owners normally hire a bookkeeper that serves as the company accountant's representative. The accountant helps the bookkeeper to perform good accounting practices and reviews his/her work periodically. (Usually on a monthly basis).

A Few Basics of Bookkeeping

Business-minded people normally have great ideas to make money, and they normally want to start their own business as early as possible. Such kinds of people don't want to waste their time doing petty things like maintaining all the records of money spent and received. They just want to make a lot of money by building their business.

Well, this can be dangerous, according to a common saying, "Haste makes waste." Business is a risky job, and without calculating the risk, anyone can fail. Planning a proper bookkeeping operation and figuring out what important financial information you want to track will play a vital role in the success of your business. With the help of proper bookkeeping, you can easily assess the performance of your business. It also provides other important information throughout the year, which can be used to formulate business strategies, choose the future direction of the business, and ensure that the business will achieve its profit-related and other overall goals.

Bookkeeping can become the most loyal partner in your business as it will help you to manage the financial assets, analyzing your liabilities, and testing your business strategies. Take proper time and attention when building an accurate and strong bookkeeping system with the help of an accountant before you make your first sale.

Choosing between the Accounting Methods

To build and maintain accounting books, you have first to ascertain how you want to record your financial transactions. In the accounting world, there are two basic accounting methods from which you have to choose one. The first one is known as the Cash-

Basis Accounting Method, and the second one is known as the Accrual Accounting Method. Both of these accounting methods differ from each other on the basis of how you record your sales and purchases in the books. In a Cash-Basis Accounting Method, a transaction is recorded when cash changes hands. In the Accrual Accounting Method, a transaction is recorded when it is completed no matter whether cash changes hands or not.

For example, if a company buys a product from a vendor to sell and doesn't pay for 30 days. In the Cash-Basis Accounting Method, this transaction is not recorded until the cash is paid to the vendor. In the Accrual Accounting Method, the transaction is recorded as purchases when the goods are received, and the future debt is recorded as Accounts Payable.

Pros and Cons of both Accounting Methods will be discussed in Chapter 2.

Assets, Liabilities, and Equity: Basic Understanding

Every business is comprised of three major financial components, which are assets, liabilities, and equity, and they should be maintained in balance. Things that the company owns are known as assets like cash, building, vehicles, land, equipment, and inventory. Liabilities are those things that the company owes to other parties like accounts payable, bills, bank loans, and bonds. Equity is the amount of capital or any other form of investment made by the owner in the business.

Introduction to Debits and Credits:

The two most important terms used in financial accounting are known as debit and credit. non-accounting personnel and non-bookkeepers normally think that debits are the subtraction of an amount from their bank accounts, and credits are the addition of an amount in their bank accounts. Well, for bookkeepers, debit and credit are a totally different concept in the world of bookkeeping. Bookkeeping involves a double-entry accounting system, which means you have to make at least two entries for any transaction (debit and credit) in your bookkeeping system. That particular transaction, whether debit or credit, adds or subtracts from an account totally depends upon the type of account.

Why you need a Chart of Accounts

You just cannot enter a transaction in any account you like. You have to analyze where exactly that particular transaction fits into the bookkeeping system. This is the time when your chart of accounts is required. Open the Chart of Accounts of your business and enter the particular transaction in the appropriate account.

Importance of Maintaining a Paper Trail

Bookkeeping is just like creating an accurate paper trail of all the financial transactions occurring throughout the year. In case of any discrepancy or any other ambiguity, you can easily track the mistake at any later date. Keeping an accurate paper trail can help you to track the financial success and failure of your business, and it also plays an important role in the growth of your business. You can assess what policies are successful so that you can repeat them, again and again, to strengthen up the internal control of your business.

All business transactions are recorded and summarized in General Ledger and Journals, which keep track of your business activities. You can make this process more effective through implementing a computerized accounting system, which can be time-saving and will provide you with the financial information of your business in different formats. You should be very careful and smart when choosing the person who will enter the financial information into the computer system and to whom you are giving access to such critical information. All these concepts will be discussed further in the following chapters.

Importance of Updating Ledger

Bookkeeping starts from a ledger, or you can say the ledger is the father of the bookkeeping system. In a ledger, you keep a summary of all your accounts and post all the financial activities that took place during the year. All the monthly, quarterly, or yearly reports are developed on the summaries of General Ledger. The information obtained from the summaries of the general ledger accounts can also be used to make key business decisions.

Posting an Entry in Journals

Small or medium-sized companies conduct hundreds of transactions each year. It is not possible to record every transaction in the General ledger as it becomes lengthy and difficult to use. As a substitute for this, most companies keep a series of journals that contain a record of activities performed in their active accounts.

For example, every company maintains a Cash Receipt Journal in which all the transactions related to cash incomings are recorded, and a Cash Disbursements Journal maintains the record of all the cash payments or outgoing cash. Other key journals of a company include purchases, sales, vendor accounts, customer accounts, and a journal of any significant activity. The creation of any journal solely depends upon the operations of the business and the need for information about the significant financial transactions.

Computerized Bookkeeping is becoming Popular

Companies are switching to computerized bookkeeping rather than maintaining their bookkeeping system on paper. The main reason behind this conversion is that it is time-saving, and computerized bookkeeping is probably more accurate.

Switching to computerized bookkeeping will not only save you time and provide you with more accuracy but will also help you to make complex reports without too much problem. These reports will further help you to make effective business decisions. The computerized accounting system has the ability to store detailed information about every transaction so that you can use them in a group to make a better business decision.

Importance of Effective Internal Controls

Strong internal control plays a vital role in the prevention and detection of fraud and also avoids the misuse of funds and other resources of the company. An effective way to build strong internal control regarding the bookkeeping system is to restrict access of an unauthorized person to the books and also avoid the flow of financial information to an irrelevant person.

You have to carefully choose the person who will receive all the cash and the person who will make cash disbursements. Make sure to allocate these duties to a separate person. This will help you to protect your business assets, theft, and fraud.

How Bookkeeping Tools Can Manage your Daily Finances

After successfully completing the process of setting up the bookkeeping system and internal controls, you are now ready to use this system, which will help you to manage your day-to-day business operations. You will definitely witness how your well-designed bookkeeping system will make your job easier to manage your business finances and help you to make effective decisions.

Inventory Control

Inventory management plays a crucial role in the success of any business. If your company maintains inventory on hand or in any warehouse, it is very important to track the cost of products so that you can manage your profits after performing respective sales. If you observe that inventory cost is getting higher, then you should adjust your prices accordingly to maintain your profit margin. In this scenario, you don't have to wait for the whole year to find out the cost of your inventory.

It is very important to keep track of your inventory. You must keep a careful watch on how much inventory you have sold and how much inventory you have left in store. Sometimes inventory gets stolen, damaged, or discarded, which means that the physical quantity of the inventory is reduced while the inventory in the books remains the same. To overcome this issue, you have to count the inventory periodically physically. Some business owners perform this activity on a monthly basis, and some with active retail stores make inventory counts on a daily basis. Another important aspect of inventory management is to maintain enough stock on hand to satisfy the demand of customers.

Maintain Record of Sales

The sales figure is the major factor that indicates the growth of any business. To get exact sales to figure on a daily basis, you have to keep your books up-to-date and accurate. This will help you to monitor the sales trend and point out individual sales figures for each product on a daily, weekly, or monthly basis.

The bookkeeping system will keep you updated about the discounts offered to customers, track the return of products and sales trends. These three elements of sales are critical when making any decisions. This will help you to formulate strategies regarding discounts, review weaknesses in sales, review pricing policy, and assess the factors that go into how sales can be increased. The cause of slow sales can be either a high price or any new competitor. In any case, you have to understand the weakness of sales and figure out ways to maintain your projected profit goals.

Tracking sales is beneficial to assess the reason for product returns. The reason might be you are providing low-quality products and need to find a new supplier. No matter what the reason is, an increase in the number of product returns is a bad sign for the business, which needs to be researched and corrected immediately.

Managing Payroll

Managing a payroll structure in a company can be tricky sometimes. Payroll requires you to follow governmental rules and regulations and maintain complete government paperwork. Your duties in managing payroll include collecting all the payroll taxes and paying employer taxes. If your company is paying employee benefits, then you have to maintain another level of record keeping.

Applying Tests for Accuracy

It is very important to make sure that the transactions you have entered are accurate. Check the process periodically to make sure the accuracy of entered transactions. According to an old saying in bookkeeping, "Garbage in, Garbage out" means that if you have entered garbage numbers in your bookkeeping system, then you will develop garbage reports from this information.

Verifying Cash

The first step in checking the accuracy of your books is to verify that all the cash transactions are recorded accurately. This can be done by checking different transactions and elements, including the cash taken by your cashier on a daily basis and the accuracy of your checking account.

Checking your Balance

After verifying the accuracy of your cash, now check that you have recorded other transactions in your books precisely. Review the accounts for any possible errors and then test the balance of them with the help of a trial balance.

Necessary Bookkeeping Corrections

There are high chances that you will not find your books balance the first time you perform a trial balance, but don't panic. On the first try, it is very rare to find your book's balance. In accounting, it is normal to make necessary adjustments at the end of an accounting period to make corrections so that the financial statements present a true and fair view of all the transactions.

Time to Celebrate your Financial Success

After completing the structure of your bookkeeping system and ensuring their balances, now it's time to celebrate the success of your efforts as now you are capable of recording financial transactions and producing reports from them. This will give you a feeling that you have put your business on the right track.

If you correctly interpret the bookkeeping information and review all the transactions made during the year, you will definitely get an idea of how well your business is doing. This will also help you to make the correct decisions, which will remove all the errors in the bookkeeping system.

Preparation of Financial Reports

Most small and medium-sized business entities prepare two financial reports at the year-end, known as a balance sheet and income statement. These two reports are commonly shown to outside people like financial institutions and to the investors from whom money is borrowed.

The Balance Sheet represents the financial position or financial strength of the business as on a particular date. A balance sheet is comprised of two sides, which balance equally. One side contains all the assets of the company, which is equal to the other side that contains the liabilities and equity of the company. This can be represented by a simple formula:

Assets = Liabilities + Equity

An income statement shows the financial performance of the company during a specific period of time. It summarizes the company's financial transactions and showcases how well the company is doing in terms of finance. In an income statement, you start by subtracting the cost of goods sold from the revenues, and then you subtract the operational expense from the remaining number. At the bottom, you will know how much profit a company has made during the specific time period. When the company has made a loss, the income statement will showcase the amount of the loss.

Paying Taxes

There is normally no obligation on small business entities to pay taxes. The profit generated from small entities is shown in the income tax returns of the owners who pay tax on it. A small business can be owned by a single person (a sole proprietorship) or a combination of two or more people running the business (a partnership). The third type of business entity is known as the company, which is incorporated as a separate legal entity whose stocks are normally purchased by the general public or investors, and they must file and pay taxes.

Chapter Two

Understanding the Basics of Bookkeeping

You will learn:

> *Business Records and their Importance*
>
> *Understanding the Accounting Cycle*
>
> *Understanding Double-Entry Bookkeeping*

All business entities, whether small or large, need to keep a record of all their financial transactions, which clearly indicates the importance of bookkeeping and bookkeepers. With having complete and accurate financial records, you can easily assess the profits and losses your business is making throughout the year.

Bookkeepers: Keepers of your Business Record

Bookkeeping is the methodology by which business entities record and track their financial transactions by following the methods of accounting. The total structure of procedures used to record, classify, and report information about financial transactions is known as Accounting. The process of bookkeeping involves recording all the financial information into the accounting system by following the accounting principles.

Bookkeepers spend most of their time ensuring that the business transactions are recorded accurately, which means that they need to be very detail-oriented. It is not compulsory that a bookkeeper should be a Certified Public Accountant (CPA). In the beginning phase of any business, most owners do their bookkeeping in order to save the salary expense of hiring someone. After some time when the business volume is increased, they hire bookkeepers or accountants who can maintain their books and prepare financial reports.

Understanding the Basic Bookkeeping Terms

It is very important to understand the bookkeeping terms before starting up with a bookkeeping system. The following is a list of terms that are common in bookkeeping and normally used on a daily basis.

Terms used in the Balance Sheet

Balance Sheet: A Balance Sheet is a financial statement that portrays the company's financial position (assets, liabilities, and equity) on a particular date. This financial statement is called the Balance Sheet because both of its sides are equally balanced, which means that the company (assets) must be equal to the claims (liabilities and equity).

A Balance Sheet is in its ideal position when its total assets are equal to the total liabilities and owner's equity. If the figures for the balance sheet fulfill this principle, then your company books are in balance.

Assets: All the tangible and intangible things, which the company owns in order to run its operations successfully, are known as assets. Assets of any company include land, building, cash, goodwill, vehicles, equipment, tools, and furniture.

Liabilities: All kinds of short-term or long-term obligations and debt owed by the company are known as liabilities such as bonds, unpaid bills, loans, debentures accounts payable, and interest payable.

Equity: All the money or any kind of asset invested in the business by the owner is known as equity. In a small or medium-sized business owned by one or more people, the equity is represented in the form of the capital account. In the incorporated company, equity is shown in the form of shares of stock. Retained earnings is another type of equity account that contains the portion of undistributed profits only held for the purpose of reinvestment. In unincorporated small businesses, the money given to the owners is paid from drawing accounts, whereas incorporated businesses distribute money to its owners (shareholders) through dividends (a portion of profit distributed among the shareholders on the basis of their ownership of shares in the company). Dividends are mostly distributed on a quarterly or yearly basis.

Terminology used in the Income Statement

Income Statement: A type of financial statement that presents the details of a company's financial activity over a certain period of time, such as a month, quarter, or year. The main purpose of an income statement is to calculate the profit/loss made by the company during a specific period of time. Income statements begin with revenue (sales made during the year) from which the cost of sales and other operating expenses are subtracted to reach the Net Profit or Loss.

Revenue: In financial terms, revenue is the type of money that is collected after selling the company's product or services. Money generated from selling the company's assets, which are no longer required, getting interested from loans issued to employees, or from any other activity, is also considered as revenue of the company.

Cost of goods sold: Money or any other resource spent on purchasing or producing the company's product or services. These products and services are used to fulfill the demand of customers.

Expense: Money spent on the operation of the company to conduct its business. Expenses are not related to the sale of goods or services.

are unit repairs an expense?

Other Common Terms

General Ledger: All the accounts of a company are summarized in a General Ledger. It is also known as the Granddaddy of the Bookkeeping system.

Accounting Period: It is the time period from which the financial information can be tracked. Some business entities track financial results on a monthly basis, so their accounting period equals one month. Some business entities track financial information on a quarterly basis, so their financial information basis on a three month period. Some business entities track financial information on a yearly basis, so their accounting period comprises 12 months. No matter how much financial information a business entity tracks, it normally presents financial data on a monthly, quarterly, and yearly basis.

Accounts Receivable: It is a type of account used to track the amount of money yet to be received from customers against the sales made on credit. In this regard, credit sales do not mean sales made through credit cards, but the sales made to customers on credit directly given by the store, which is receivable on any later date.

Accounts payable: The account used to ascertain the outstanding amount against bills from vendors, consultants, contractors, or from individuals or from companies from whom products or services were received.

Depreciation: Depreciation is an accounting method used to reduce the value of an asset depending upon its usage and age. For example, if you own a vehicle for use, it is obvious that its value will be reduced with the passing of each year. This rule is applicable to all the assets of the business. Business assets are used regularly and age with the passage of time and need replacement after a certain period of time. Key assets like vehicle, building, equipment, machinery, furniture, and other assets depreciate with time and need replacement.

Interest: Interest is the amount of money payable by the company to the lenders of funds. A company can borrow money from commercial banks, financial institutions, or individuals who offer lending services for money. For example, when you purchase a car using a car loan facility, then you have to pay the borrowed money with a fixed percentage of interest on borrowed money.

Trial Balance: Trial Balance gives you the surety that the books are balanced before pulling out information for preparing financial reports.

Payroll: The procedure of payment to the employees. Maintaining payroll is a crucial function in the bookkeeping system as it involves different aspects of reporting like taxes to be paid on behalf of the employee, workman's compensation, and unemployment taxes.

Journals: In Journals, bookkeepers maintain records of daily company transactions. Records of most active company accounts are maintained like Accounts Receivable, Accounts Payable, Cash, and other key accounts. These all accounts have their own separate journals.

Inventory: Account that tracks record of a closing stock and all products that will be sold to customers.

Stepping through the Accounting Cycle

Bookkeepers complete the work through completing the tasks of the accounting cycle. All the workflow is in a circular flow, which is why it is called the accounting cycle. The whole process starts with entering a transaction, keep flowing the transaction through the accounting cycle, closing the books at the end of the accounting period and then again starting the whole task from the beginning for the next accounting period.

The complete Accounting Cycle consists of eight steps.

1. **Transactions:** The process of accounting cycle starts from a financial transaction. Transactions can include the purchase of supplies for business activities, sales or sales return of products from customers, or any other business activity that involves an exchange of the company's asset, payment of debt or expense, or drawings made by the company's owner. All such activities of

the business are known as transactions, and they should be recorded whenever they take place.

2. **Journal Entries:** Recording of transactions in an appropriate journal through maintaining the chronological order of transactions. It is the first place where the transaction is recorded and is also known as the "Book of Original Entry."

3. **Posting:** Entering the transactions into the accounts, which get the impact. These accounts are the parts of the General ledger, which contains a summary of all the business's accounts.

4. **Trail Balance:** You can verify the accuracy of the bookkeeping system through checking the balance of the Trial Balance at the end of the accounting period (which can be a month, quarter, or a year depending on the business operations).

5. **Worksheet:** Most of the time, your first calculations of the trial balance will show that your books are not balanced. In such a scenario, it is obvious to look for errors to make corrections called adjustments, which are tracked on a worksheet.

6. **Adjusting Journal Entries:** Adjustments are only made when the trial balance indicates that after making necessary adjustments in the account, errors in the trial balance can be rectified. You don't need to make any adjustments before the process of the trial balance is completed and clearly indicates the requirement of corrections and adjustments.

7. **Financial Statement:** After making necessary adjustments in the accounts, now is the time to prepare the balance sheet and income statement using corrected account balances.

8. **Closing:** Close the books after completing the accounting period and get a net balance of every account. Now begin the entire cycle of accounting again with opening balances for the next year.

A businessman always wants to monitor the performance of his business through profit or loss on month-by-month, quarter-by-quarter and year-by-year basis. For this purpose, Revenue and Expense accounts must start with a zero balance each accounting year. On the other hand, account balances of various accounts like assets, accounts receivable, accounts payable will have some balance at the beginning of the year because you cannot replace every asset each year or can pay all the creditors at the end of the year and start the year with a zero balance. In these accounts, the process of payment and collection continues, and it is very rare that these accounts show zero balance.

Choosing between the Cash-Basis or Accrual Accounting System

There are basically two major accounting systems for the purpose of recording a transaction. You have to choose between Cash-Basis or Accrual Accounting system to record a transaction. The main difference between both systems is how you record your financial transactions.

Cash-Basis Accounting require real-time Cash Movement

In the Cash-Basis accounting system, you are bound to record the transaction in the books when cash actually changes hands. This means that when cash is paid by the company for supplies or when cash is received from customers against providing products or services. Cash payments and receipts can be in the form of a check, cash, credit card payment, electronic fund transfer, or any other means used for the payment of any item.

Sales made on store credit facilities are not recorded in the cash-basis accounting system. In a cash-basis accounting system, there is no obligation to track or record sales made to customers on a credit basis. The same goes for purchases, as well. Only those items are recorded in the books whose payment is made through cash, no matter whether the supplies are stored for later sales purposes. In case the supplies are purchased on credit terms, this transaction will not be recorded in the books until the cash is paid.

When you need to monitor and gauge the cash flow in a company, you need to use the cash-basis accounting system. This is one of the best methods to measure the revenues earned. You will also get to know the expenses of the company. Let's study the cash-basis system with an example. Suppose that you buy a different product in June for $2000. Due to the volatile market, you do not get a buyer for these products in June and have to retain the products until July. When you make up the books for the month, they will show an expense of $2000 and no revenue. This clearly indicates a loss in that month. When the same products are sold in July for $ 2,500, it will show a profit of $ 2,500 in the month of July. When you make the monthly report, you will see a loss of $2,000 in the month of June and a profit of $ 2,500 in the month of July, but in reality, you had made a profit of $ 500 over a two-month period.

Method of Recording in Accrual Accounting System

In the Accrual Accounting system, bookkeepers record all transactions when they occur, even without the movement of cash from one hand to another. For example, if you made sales on store credit, you immediately post an entry in the accounts receivable without receiving any cash. If you made purchases from the supplier without paying cash, you enter the amount of the accounts payable account until you pay out the cash.

Accrual accounting system has its own drawbacks. This system of accounting is good for matching revenues and expenses but is not very effective in tracking cash flow. This is because you increased your revenue when you made the sales even without receiving any cash, and this will make the income statement impressive while, in reality, you don't have any cash in your bank against that particular sale. For example, if you are running a business on a contractual basis, you will record revenue when the contract is completed even without receiving any cash payment. If your customers are paying you at a slow pace, then at the end of an accounting period, you will show a huge revenue with little cash. The only method to tackle slow-paying customers is to manage accounts receivable so that you can avoid the cash-shortage problem.

Companies that follow the accrual accounting system closely monitor the cash flow on a weekly basis to make sure that the company has enough cash on hand to perform business operations. If you are running a seasonal business like tourism, then you can face cash-flow problems in winter due to slow or no work, to overcome this issue, you can contact your bank and apply for a short-term credit facility to maintain a constant flow of cash during slow months.

Double-Entry Bookkeeping System

No matter which accounting method - cash-basis or accrual accounting system - you implement in your business for the purpose of bookkeeping, you have to use double-entry bookkeeping to maintain your books. This transaction entry system will help you to minimize errors and increase the chances of your books being balanced. In this system, each transaction is entered twice; that is why it is called a double-entry bookkeeping system. The formula of a balance sheet (Assets = Liabilities + Capital) plays a vital role in the double-entry bookkeeping system.

To maintain the balance in the world of bookkeeping, a combination of debits and credits are used. People normally think that debit is subtraction as it reduces the balance from their bank accounts, and credits are an addition as unexpected credits in their bank accounts increase their balance. Forget these concepts of debits and credits, as they have a totally different meaning in the world of bookkeeping.

In the bookkeeping world, the definite thing about debit and credit is that debit comes on the left side of a transaction while a credit appears on the right side of a transaction. You will get confused to see anything beyond that. This can be explained through an example.

Suppose you have purchased a table for office use that costs $ 1000. This single transaction can be divided into two parts: You spend an asset (cash) to buy another asset (furniture). This means that you have to update two accounts in your books, Furniture Account and Cash Account. The method to enter this transaction is shown below.

Account Debit Credit

Furniture $1,000

Cash $1,000

To purchase a new desk for the office.

Relevant accounts are adjusted, which are impacted by the above transaction. Furniture account is increased though a debit as furniture is added, and a cash account is decreased through credit as it is cash is outflow in the form of payment. In this transaction, both accounts of asset sides are impacted, so we have to look at the changes in the balance sheet.

Assets = Liabilities + Capital

Furniture increase = payment is made through cash

Cash decreases = Assets are increased

One asset is increased by sacrificing another asset. This means there will be no effect on the balance sheet, and both of its sides will give the same figures.

This is another example of a transaction that will show you an impact on both sides of the balance sheet equation. Suppose that you have purchased supplies in the amount of $ 5000 on credit. This particular transaction will increase your inventory as well as your accounts payable. Remember that accounts payable is the account used to track the funds, which are yet to be paid in future, time. This transaction will be recorded as:

Account Debit Credit

Inventory $5,000

Accounts Payable $5,000

To purchase widgets for sale to customers.

Effect on a balance sheet is shown below:

   Assets = Liabilities + Equity

Accounts payable increases = Inventory increases (No change in both sides)

Both of these two examples have clearly shown how double-entry bookkeeping systems maintain the balance of your books. Balancing books may look simple and easy when there are times when they became complicated when more than two accounts are involved in a single transaction. But don't panic now; you'll learn all the concepts gradually and will become an expert in maintaining the books of your business.

[handwritten: how does company overhead get balanced - or payroll?]

Principles of differentiating between Debits and Credits

Debits and Credits in the bookkeeping system are totally different from the general concepts. You have to memorize these general principles of debits and credits for passing correct and accurate journal entries. All the accounting system revolves around five major accounts. Try to understand the ways of treating these accounts.

1. **Assets Account:** Assets are debit whenever they are increased, and when assets are decreased, they fall on the credit side.

2. Liabilities: Decrease in liability will be a debit, while an increase in the liability makes it a credit.

3. Income: Whenever the income decreases, you will debit it, and when the income starts increasing, you will make a credit.

4. Expenses: Increase in expenses are treated on the debit side while the decrease in expenses falls on the credit side.

5. Capital: Increase in the capital will be credited while the decrease in the capital (in the form of drawings) will be debited.

Chapter Three

How Charts of Accounts Ease doing Financial Planning

You will learn:

    Get to know the Chart of Accounts

    Understanding Different Types of Accounts

    How to make the Accounts for the Company

Just imagine the complication and mess when you forgot to record the payment made through the checkbook. If you don't maintain the record of cash outflow and inflow from your bank account, then there are chances of the check bouncing, and you can miss an important payment on time.

Maintaining a checkbook is much easier than keeping the books of business. Every business transaction must be recorded carefully to make sure that it enters into the right account. Careful bookkeeping is an effective tool to measure the financial performance of a business.

Bookkeeping is a complete process that follows a cycle. This means that to maintain accurate books, you need a roadmap that will help you to determine where to record a transaction. The Chart of Accounts will be your roadmap. The Chart of accounts includes many different types of accounts, which can help you to track the key parts of any business, like assets, liabilities, expenses, revenue, and equity.

Introduction of Charts of Accounts

It is compulsory to record every business transaction in its appropriate account so that you can track it in the future. Charts of Accounts are the roadmap created by the business to organize its financial transactions. You can only record a transaction when you know where to put it, and charts of accounts show you that direction. Each account has its own description, which informs you of its type and purpose of recording a transaction. It is rarely possible that you find two businesses with the same Charts of Accounts. Some businesses have similarities in Charts of Accounts on the basis of organizational and structural characteristics. All the organization and its structure are designed to present two major financial reports: the balance sheet, which shows the financial strength/position of the company, and the income statement that shows how much profit/loss the company has made during a specific accounting period.

You can initiate your Chart of Accounts from the Balance Sheet, which includes:

Current Assets: the most liquid forms of things that can be used in a period of 12 months are known as liquid assets such as inventory, cash, bank, and accounts receivable.

Fixed Assets: Include all things owned by a company that has a lifespan of more than 12 months. Fixed assets take time for conversion into cash, such as vehicles, land, building, equipment, and furniture.

Current Liabilities: Track all accounts of debt which need to be discharged by a company in the next 12 months such as accounts payable, interest payable, bills payable, and credit card payments.

Long-term Liabilities: Track all accounts of debt, which can be paid after 12 months, such as bonds payable, mortgages payable, and debentures.

Equity: Tracks all the money invested in the business by the owner or claims of the owner in the company's assets. The profit, which is reinvested in the business, also falls into account of equity.

Income Statement Chart of Accounts include:

Revenue: Tracks all accounts that generate money after making sales of the company's product or services or from any other source.

Cost of Goods Sold: It includes all those accounts, which accumulate direct costs incurred in the selling of the company's products or services.

Expenses: Tracks all accounts, which involve the outflow of money for the purpose of running business operations, related to making sales of the company's products or services.

Charts of Accounts are developed after listing all the Liability accounts, Asset accounts, the equity accounts, the revenue accounts, and the expense accounts. The Balance Sheet and Income Statement are the two places where all these accounts come.

The purpose of making a Chart of Accounts is to manage the flow of money effectively. So, it is very important to prepare a chart of accounts carefully as it will provide the financial information which can be used to make smart business decisions. You can add new accounts during the year, but it is recommended that if you want to delete any account, wait for the end of a 12-month reporting period.

Explaining Balance Sheet Accounts

The Balance Sheet is the first part of the Chart of Accounts. A balance sheet can be further categorized into three parts, as shown below:

Asset: Asset accounts are used to trace all the items and things owned by the company, such as land, building, equipment, vehicles, furniture, and so on.

Liabilities: Liability accounts are used to track all the obligations of the business, including claims made by lenders against the assets of the company such as loans, mortgages, and similar types of credits.

Equity: Money or any other type of resource invested in the business by the owner is tracked from the equity account.

Balance Sheet accounts and the financial reports made from these should balance out. The total value of assets must be equal to the combined total value of liabilities and equity.

Treatment of Different Assets

A first and primary account in the Chart of Accounts is the asset account that contains all items, which a company owns. Asset accounts can be further classified into the current asset and long-term assets.

Cash in Hand: Petty cash kept in the office or at the retail store outlet to meet the daily need can be traced from this account. A small portion of the cash amount is kept at the retail store registers to provide change to the customers. The same is the case in offices; petty cash is used to fulfill the immediate cash requirements.

Cash in Operation: This is the primary account of any company, which is used to perform a business operation and is also known as checking account. This account is used to pay expenses and to deposit revenue. Companies that have more than one division for conducting their operations may have more than one checking account.

Cash in Savings: Surplus cash funds that have no immediate use are deposited into the savings account for a certain period of time to earn interest money. In the meantime, the company decides what to do with the surplus funds.

Accounts Receivable: When the customer bought your products or services at the store credit facility, then you have to keep the record of the amount receivable from customers. This account will help in tracking all the money due to customers. Products sold on a credit card are not entered into this account because you will receive the money from the bank on behalf of the customer.

Inventory: This account informs you about the products in hand available for sale to your customers. The value of stock mainly depends upon the method on which you record your inventory and how it flows in and out.

Prepaid Insurance: This account is used to track the amount of money paid in advance against the insurance. For example, you have purchased an insurance plan for one year for a building. You will credit the whole amount and reduce it by a ratio of 1/12 each month.

You can set up a variety of other accounts depending upon the nature and requirement of your business. For example, if you are running a barter asset business (business in which things are exchanged for other things), then you can add a Barter Account. If you are offering consulting services, then you can add up a Consulting account to track your cash collected from providing consulting services.

Fixed/Long-Term Assets

Long-term assets are normally those types of assets owned by the company with the intention of using them for more than 12-months and are not readily converted into cash. A company can own a list of long-term assets, but key accounts are the factory, land, and building.

Land: This account maintains the record of land owned by the company. You can put the value of the land on the basis of its purchase cost. Land and building value are tracked separately as land doesn't depreciate its value while the building depreciates. Depreciation is an accounting method used to reduce the value of assets after being used.

Building: The value of a building is tracked through this account. Just like land, building an initial value is based on its purchasing cost. To ascertain the accurate value of building each year, a predetermined rate of depreciation is applied to the building.

Leasehold Improvements: A company may acquire buildings or land on lease terms and spend money on improvements to increase its valve. This account tracks all the money spent on leasehold assets. When a company acquires any land on lease, it may spend money to make improvements of the property to make it usable according to needs. For example, when a company leases a store in a mall, it will be an empty hall, and the company has to spend money on shelves and other improvements to decorate it according to its needs.

Vehicles: This account tracks all vehicles owned by a company like a car, motorbikes, trucks, vans, etc. The value of vehicles is recorded at the amount paid the time of purchasing it plus any additional cost incurred by the company. For example, if the company is providing services to handicapped people, then the company has to make a few adjustments to the van to make it usable for the handicapped people. Like other assets, vehicles also undergo the process of depreciation.

Equipment: All the equipment purchased by the company for use for more than one year is tracked in this account, such as cash registers, computers, copiers, and tools. The valve of equipment is recorded on the basis of their purchase price and are depreciated over the period of their use. Depreciation is necessary for equipment as they indicate their age and show the time for their replacement.

Furniture and Fixture: This account tracks all the furniture and fixture owned by the company, such as tables, chairs, shelves, office desks, cupboards, etc. The value of the company's furniture and fixtures is recorded at the amount of their purchase cost and depreciated on a yearly basis during their useful lifespan.

Accumulated Depreciation: This account tracks the amount of total depreciation faced by the company's asset.

Now, we will look toward the value of those long-term assets, which are not present in a physical form but are still valuable for the company in terms of money such as copyrights, goodwill, and organizational costs. These assets are known as "Intangible Assets" and include the following accounts:

Organizational Costs: This account tracks all the expenses incurred to start-up a new business which can't be written off in the first year such legal expense fees or obtaining a special license. To write off these special expenses, a company spreads them over future years using a special method known as "amortization."

Patents: This account is used to track all the costs incurred in obtaining patents or any government grants. Patents are exclusive rights issued by the government to the inventor of products or services for a certain period of time. The value of the asset includes the cost incurred in getting the patent rights. The cost of patent rights is amortized, just like organizational cost.

Goodwill: This account is needed to ascertain the value of a company based on its reputation, store location, and customer base. When a company buys another company and pays more money than its tangible assets, than the excess money indicates the value of its goodwill.

Copyrights: This account tracks all the costs incurred in obtaining the copyright, legal rights given to a publisher, playwright, an author, or any other distributor or publisher for the production of work like music, literature, art, or drama. The authorized rights expire after a number of years, so its value is amortized with each passing year.

Amortization: Amortization is the process, just like depreciation used to write off the value of intangible goods. This account tracks all the costs accumulated after getting the intangible assets amortized.

There are some assets owned by the company, which doesn't carry too much value or are not regularly used in the business operations. Such assets fall in the category of "Other Assets." Any type of asset from other assets that you want to track individually can be shifted to its own account later on.

Streamline Your Liabilities

After setting the list of assets owned by your company, now is the time to streamline all the accounts, which your business owes to others. A business can owe money to the supplier of raw material, financial institutions, or to any person or institution that offers money-lending services. Just like assets, liabilities can be classified into current liabilities and long-term liabilities.

Current Liabilities: Liabilities, which the company is bound to discharge within a period of 12-months, are known as current liabilities. Most common accounts of current liabilities that appear in the chart of accounts are:

Accounts Payable: This account tracks all debt/money payable by the company to the vendors, suppliers, and contractors in less than a year's time. Most of the payment must be paid in a 30-90 days period from the initial billing time.

Credit Cards Payable: Account use to track outstanding credit card payments. Most companies use credit card facilities to meet short-term payment needs, which are paid off at the end of each month. Carrying a credit card balance payment for a longer time period can result in facing high-interest payments like credit cards.

Sales Tax collected: Companies are permitted to collect sales tax on products or services on behalf of the government. This account is used to track all the accumulated money collected in the form of sales tax. Companies then pay collected sales tax money to the government authorities on a monthly basis.

Accrued Payroll Taxes: Money collected in the form of payroll taxes, medical taxes, social security taxes are tracked in this account. Companies don't need to pay these taxes on an immediate basis and mostly submit these taxes to the government on a monthly or quarterly basis. This account is maintained to keep the record of such money.

Above are the most common type of accounts used in the current liabilities portion of the balance sheet. There is no restriction of using more accounts in a category. It all depends upon how you want to manage your business operations and how much detail you want.

Long-term Liabilities:

Long-term liabilities are a type of debt that can be paid after the 12-months period. On the basis of your debt structure, you can maintain your accounts in the chart of accounts. Loans payable and Notes payable are the two most common types of account maintained in long-term liabilities:

Loans Payable: These accounts maintain the amount of money taken against collateral. Mortgages are a long-term loan obtained against a building. Some companies maintain separate accounts for each loan obtained, like a vehicle loan or simple loan payable.

Notes Payable: Companies may borrow money from other businesses using notes. In this method, no asset is placed as collateral against the loan obtained. This account is used to track all the money due in the form of notes payable.

Any separate long-term debt can be calculated in the "Other Liabilities" account. In case that loan account becomes prominent and needs to be tracked individually, you can allocate it to a separate account.

Allocation of Equity

Every business is treated as a separate entity in the business world. You can say that a business is a process, which is always owned by somebody. An owner makes a contribution in the form of money and assets to initiate a business. The equity account tracks the owner's contribution to the business as well as the portion of his ownership. The ownership of businesses running in the form of corporations is tracked through the share of stocks while the businesses in the form of sole proprietorship and partnership, ownership is determined through capital or drawings account. Some prominent accounts of equity presented in the chart of accounts are discussed below:

Common Stock: This account tracks the amount of money received after issuing a share of the company. The total value of issued shares is obtained by multiplying the share issued with the value of each share. Only the company form of business maintains this account.

Retained Earnings: This account is used to track all the profit and loss made by the coming from the beginning of its operations. If the company has made a profit during the year, that certain amount is added into the account, and in case of loss, that amount is subtracted. For example, if the income statement shows a profit of $ 500,000, then the amount is added into the retained earnings account, and if it shows a loss of $ 500,000, then the amount is subtracted from the retained earnings.

Capital: Capital account is mostly maintained by the sole-proprietorship or partnership type of business. This account keeps the record of money invested by the owner at the beginning of the business, and additional money contributed when the business requires it. Capital account also keeps the record of other assets invested in the business by the owner like building, car, equipment, tools and etc. If the business is owned by more than one person, than each partner can get his/her own capital account to track their contributions.

Drawings: Unincorporated type of businesses usually maintains drawings account. This account is used to track all the money taken out of business by the owners. If the business is owned by more than one person, than each partner can get his/her own drawing account.

Accounts Presented on the Income Statement

The income statement is used to present the profit or loss; the business has made during the year after successfully conducting its operations. There are mainly two accounts an Income statement is comprised of:

Revenue: This account tracks all the money coming into the business in the form of income, such as money received after selling the company's products and services, interest earned on savings, or from any other source of income.

Expenses: Account used to track all the money spent on operations, which keeps the business running smoothly.

Keeping Record of Money you Make

Sales of Goods or Services: Money generated particularly after selling the company's products or services or a combination of both. This account is used to track all that money.

Sales Discounts: To boost up sales figures and to maintain customer loyalty, many companies offer discounts at selling prices. This reduction in selling price is maintained in this account.

Sales Return: Sometimes, customers become unhappy with the purchased product and want to return it back. This account is used to keep the record of all the returned merchandises.

Other Income: A company can generate income from a source other than its primary activity of selling goods or services such as interest earned on an investment, sale of a fixed asset, or from any other source. This account is used to track all such income received from any other source.

Tracking Cost of Sales

It is obvious that you have to spend some money on manufacturing or to buy any product which can be further sold to make money. The cost of sales is the account used to track money spent on such activities. Common accounts used in the Cost of sales are:

Purchases: This account maintains the record of all the item, which you used to buy from vendors or from the supplier in order to make sales to your customers.

Purchase Discount: If you pay the money on time or at the time of purchase, then there are high chances of getting a discount. This account is used to track all the discounts availed at the time of purchasing. For example, a company can get a 2% discount on a gross amount if the payment is made within 10 days of getting the initial bill.

Purchase returns: If you are not satisfied with the product you have purchased, then record the value of the product, you have returned to the supplier.

Freight Charges: Money paid to get the items delivered at your warehouse from the supplier's location is recorded in this account.

Maintaining a Record of the Money you Spend

To run the business smoothly, you have to make different expenses. These all expenses are not tied directly with sales of the business but helps in providing assistance to run the operations smoothly. There is a large list of expenses that a company has to make and can be tracked through their separate accounts. Chart of Accounts shows your business operations, and so you have to decide how much detail you want from your business. You can make as many expense account as you want, but the most common expense account, which is mostly used in every business, is discussed below.

Advertising: This account is used to keep track of money spent on promoting business activities or its products. Advertising expense includes money spent on newspaper, magazines, television, printing flyers, branding, publishing catalogs, and mailings to customers. The cost of participating in any social activity like walk, organizing seminars also falls in the advertising expense account.

Bank service charges: Charges deducted by the bank against providing its services to the company are tracked from this account.

Rental Expense: A company may obtain any equipment, building, vehicle, or any other asset to the rental agreement. All the money paid in the form of rent is tracked from this account. These assets are mostly obtained for a short period of time.

Insurance: Money spent to buy insurance is tracked from this account. Many companies bought the insurance and made a separate account for each type of insurance like employee insurance, car insurance, building insurance, machinery insurance, and many more. In case of any unfortunate event, insurance money is used to cover the expenses.

Legal and Accounting: Sometimes, companies may seek advisory services from accounting and legal firms. The money spent on these services is tracked from this account.

Miscellaneous Expenses: There are few expenses that need to incur but don't fall in the expense account. So, the companies establish a miscellaneous expense account to track all the money spent on such activities. You can be very careful when the passing entry in these accounts as a double recording of expense can cause the error.

Office expense: In order to run the office smoothly, you have to bear some expenses like stationery, supplies, and office equipment. All office expenses are tracked from this account. If you think that your office is using more amount of paper than usual, than you can establish a separate account for office paper.

Payroll Taxes: This account maintains the record of all the funds deducted from employees' monthly pay under the instructions of the government, such as Medicare, social security, unemployment compensation, and workman's compensation. The company is bound to pay these funds to the government on a monthly basis.

Rent Expense: Money paid in the form of rent by the company is tracked in this account. A company obtained office space, building, or a factory on a rental basis.

Salaries and Wages: This account is used to track the money paid to employees in the form of salaries and wages.

Utilities: Utility account keeps the record of all the payments made in terms of using electricity, gas, and water.

Establishing Chart of Accounts

Choose from the list of accounts discussed above to set up your own Chart of Accounts for your business. There is no restriction or secret in making your own chart of accounts. Just choose those accounts, which are necessary for the operations of your business.

Don't panic when setting up a chart of accounts for the first. People normally have no idea what type of accounts will be suitable for their business. Choose any accounts and establish your chart of accounts, and if you feel necessary, you can add an account in your chart at any time. The chart of Accounts normally includes three main columns:

Account: Includes the name of the account.

Types: Include the type of accounts such as asset, liability, equity, income, cost of sales, and expense.

Description: Provide basic information about the transaction, which is recorded in the account.

Large companies, which maintain hundreds of accounts, mostly allot number to each account. If your company is using a computerized system, then the computer will automatically assign numbers to your accounts. For manual records, you have to assign a number on your own. A most common number system is as follows:

Asset accounts: 100 to 999

Liabilities account: 1,000 to 1,999

Equity accounts: 2,000 to 2,999

Sales and cost of goods sold accounts: 3,000 to 3,999

Expense accounts: 4,000 to 4,999

This is only an example of giving numbers to various accounts. You can assign your own numbering system to your accounts.

Chapter Four

Ledgers: Record of Business Transactions

You will learn:

   Know what a General Ledger Is

   How to Develop a Ledger

   Adjusting the Ledger Entries

A person who maintains the record of things needs a source to track everything. Just like this, bookkeepers always want a source from which they can track each and every financial transaction, which they have recorded. General Ledger is a blessing for a bookkeeper, as it presents a summarized description of every transaction the business has made.

Source of Information for a Business

General Ledger of a business is also known as the eyes and ears of business as every information passes through it. In any case, wouldn't it be decent if the record could simply disclose everything to you what comes in and out from the business? That would absolutely be easier to find any accounting issues or mistake.

General Ledger plays the role of eyes and ears for clerks and bookkeepers that need it to realize what money related exchanges have occurred in business. By perusing General Ledger — not actually fascinating perusing except if you love numbers — you can see, account by account, each exchange that has occurred in the business.

General Ledger is the granddaddy of your business. You can discover every transaction that occurred at any point throughout the entire existence of the business in the General Ledger account. It's the one spot where you can discover transactions that involve Cash, Inventory, Accounts Receivable, Accounts Payable, and some other record incorporated into your business' Chart of Accounts.

How to make Entries in the Ledger

Every business's transactions are first entered into journals; you create a large number of the entries for General Ledger according to the information obtained from journals. For instance, money receipts and the accounts that are affected by those receipts are recorded in the Cash Receipts journal. Money payment and the accounts affected by those payments are recorded in the Cash Payment Journal. The same is applicable for transactions found in the Sales Journal, a Purchases journal, General Journal, and some other uncommon journals, which you might find important for your business.

At the end of every month, you summarize every journal by including the segments and develop that outline to build up a section for General Ledger. Trust me; it will take much less time than entering each transaction in General Ledger.

Account	Debit	Credit
Cash	$2,900	
Accounts Receivable		$500
Sales		$900
Capital		$1,500

In the above transaction, Debits and Credits are in balance — $2,900 each. Keep in mind all sections to General Ledger must be adjusted equally. That is the basic and most important guideline of the double-entry bookkeeping system.

In this example, the Cash account is increased by $2,900 to show that money was received. The Accounts Receivable account is decreased by $500 to show clients have made their payments. The Sales account is increased by $900, in light of the fact that extra income was generated. The Capital account is increased by $1,500 in light of the fact that the owner has invested more money into the business.

Another example of passing entry in the general ledger is shown below:

Account

Accounts Receivable

Debit

$800

Credit

Sales

$800

In the above example, the accounts receivable account is increased by $ 800 after making a sale on credit to customers. The sales account is increased by $ 800 as the company has generated revenue after selling its products or services.

Methods of Posting Entries into the Ledger

When posting on General Ledger, incorporate exchange dollar sums just as references to where the material was initially gone into the books so you can follow an exchange back if an inquiry emerges later. For instance, you may consider what a number methods, your chief or the proprietor may ask why certain cash was spent, or an inspector (an outside bookkeeper who checks your work for exactness) could bring up an issue

Whatever the explanation somebody is scrutinizing a passage in General Ledger, you certainly need to have the option to discover the purpose of a unique section for each exchange in each record. Utilize the reference data that aides you to where the first insight concerning the exchange is situated in the diaries to respond to any scrutinize that emerges.

For this specific business, three of the records — Cash, Accounts Receivable, and Accounts Payable — are continued month to month, so every ha an opening equalization. Just to keep things basic, in this model

Most organizations close their books toward the finish of every month and do monetary reports. Others close them toward the finish of a quarter or end of a year. For the motivations behind this model, I accept that this business shuts its books month to month. Furthermore, in the figures that pursue, I just give models for the initial five days of the month to keep things basic.

As you survey the figures for the different records in this model, pay heed that the parity of certain records increment when a charge is recorded and decline when credit is recorded. Others increment when credit is recorded and decline when a charge is recorded. That is the puzzle of charges, credits, and twofold passage bookkeeping.

The Cash account (see Figure 4-5) increments with charges and diminishes with credits. In a perfect world, the Cash account consistently finishes with a charge balance, which implies there's still cash in the record. A credit balance in the money account demonstrates that the business is overdrawn, and you recognize what that implies — checks are returned for delinquency.

Adjustments Made to Rectify Errors in the Ledger

Your entrances in General Ledger aren't thrown in stone. On the off chance that important, you can generally change or address a passage with what's called a modifying section. Four of the most widely recognized explanations behind General Ledger changes are:

Depreciation: A business shows the maturing of its advantages through appreciation. Every year, a part of the first cost of a benefit is discounted as a cost, and that change is noted as an altering section. Deciding what amount ought to be discounted is a convoluted procedure that I clarify in more noteworthy detail in Chapter 12.

Prepaid costs: Expenses that are paid in advance, for example, a year of protection, are allotted continuously utilizing a modifying passage. This sort of modifying passage is typically done as a component of the end procedure toward the finish of a bookkeeping period. I tell you the best way to create sections identified with prepaid costs in Chapter 17.

Adding a record: Accounts can be included by method for altering sections whenever during the year. On the off chance that the new record is being made to follow exchanges independently that once showed up in another record, you should move all exchanges as of now in the books to the new record.

You do this exchange with an altering section to mirror the change.

Deleting a record: Accounts should just be erased toward the finish of a bookkeeping period. I show you the sort of passages you have to make in General Ledger beneath.

None of this chapter makes sense & it is in desperate need of an editor!

Chapter Five

Maintaining Journals

You will learn:

Making Journals with a Single Entry

Tracking the Purchases, Sales, and Cash

Posting these Entries in Accounts

When it comes to doing your books, you should begin someplace. You could take an alternate way and simply list each exchange in the influenced accounts, however in the wake of recording hundreds and possibly a large number of exchange in only one month, envision what a bad dream you'd face if your books didn't adjust and you needed to discover the mistake. It would resemble searching for a needle in a bundle — a pile of numbers!

Since you enter each exchange in two spots — that is, like a charge in one record and a credit in another record — in a twofold passage accounting framework, you have to have a spot where you can without much of a stretch match those charges and credits.

Sometime in the past, accountants built up an arrangement of diaries to give organizations a beginning stage for every exchange. In this part, we acquaint you with the procedure of journalizing your exchanges; we disclose to you how to set up and use diaries, how to present the exchanges on accounts affected, and how to simplify this whole procedure by utilizing an electronic accounting program.

Prepare Transaction's Point of Entry

In many organizations that don't utilize mechanized accounting programs, an exchange's unique purpose of passage into the accounting framework is through an arrangement of diaries.

Every exchange goes in the fitting diary in sequential requests.

The passage ought to incorporate data about the date of the exchange, the records to which the exchange was posted, and the source material utilized for building up the exchange.

On the off chance that, sooner or later, you have to follow how a credit or charge wound up in a specific record, you can locate the essential detail in the diary where you initially posted the exchange. (Before it's presented on different records in the accounting framework, every exchange gets a reference number to assist you with backtracking to the first passage point.) For instance, assume a client calls you and needs to know why his record has a $500 charge. To discover the appropriate response, you go to the posting in the client's record, track the chargeback to its unique purpose of section in the Sales diary, utilize that data to find the hotspot for the charge, make a duplicate of the source (no doubt a business receipt or receipt), and mail the proof to the client.

In the event that you've recorded everything appropriately, you ought to experience no difficulty finding the first source material and settling any issue that emerges with respect to any trans-activity.

It's impeccably satisfactory to keep one general diary for every one of your exchanges; however, one major diary can be difficult to oversee on the grounds that you'll like have thou-sands of passages in that diary before the year's over. Rather, most organizations utilize an arrangement of diaries that incorporates a Cash Receipts diary for approaching money and a Cash Disbursement diary for active money. Not all exchanges include money, notwithstanding, so the two most regular non-money diaries are the Sales diary and the Purchases diary. I tell you the best way to set up and utilize every one of these diaries in the segments that pursue.

Movement of Cash

Organizations manage money exchanges each day, and as an entrepreneur, you certainly need to know where each penny is going. The ideal approach to get a snappy day-by-day outline of money exchanges is by assessing the sections in your Cash Receipts diary and Cash Disbursements journal.

Maintain Record of Cash Inflows

The Cash Receipts diary is the primary spot you record money got by your business. Most of the money got every day originates from day by day deals; other potential wellsprings of money incorporate stores of capital from the company's proprietor, client charge installments, new advance continues, and enthusiasm from bank accounts.

Every section in the Cash Receipts diary must demonstrate how the money was gotten as well as assign the record into which the money will be kept. Keep in mind, in twofold section accounting; each exchange is entered twice — once as a charge and once as a credit.

For instance, money taken in for deals is credited to the Sales record and charged to the Cash account. For this situation, the two records increment in esteem.

In the Cash Receipts diary, the Cash account is consistently the charge since it's the place you at first store your cash. The credits differ contingent on the wellspring of the assets. Figure 5-1 gives you what a progression of exchanges resemble when they're gone into a Cash Receipts diary.

You record the vast majority of your approaching money every day since it is money received by the clerk, and called sales to register sales or just deals in the diary. At the point when you record checks received from clients, you list the client's check number and name as well as the sum.

The Cash Receipts diary has seven sections of data:

Date: The date of the exchange.

Account Credited: The name of the record credited.

PR (post reference): Where the exchange will be posted toward the month's end. This data is filled in toward the month's end when you do the presenting on the General Ledger accounts. In the event that the section to be presented on the records is condensed and totaled at the base of the page, you can simply put a checkmark by the passage in the PR segment. For exchanges recorded in the General Credit or General Debit sections, you ought to demonstrate a record number for the record into which the trans-activity is posted.

General Credit: Transactions that don't have their very own sections; these exchanges are entered separately into the records affected.

Accounts Receivable Credit: Any exchanges that are presented on the Accounts Receivable record (which tracks data about customers who purchase items on store credit).

Sales Credit: Credits for the Sales account.

Cash Debit: Anything that will be added to the Cash account.

You can set up your Cash Receipts diary with more segments in the event that you have accounts with visit money receipts. The enormous bit of leeway to having singular segments for dynamic records is that, when you absolute the sections toward the month's end, the aggregate for the dynamic records is the main thing you need to add to the General Ledger accounts, which is significantly less work at that point entering each deal exchange separately in the General Ledger account. This methodology spares a great deal of time, presenting on accounts that include numerous exchanges each month. Singular exchanges recorded in the General Credits section each should be gone into the influenced records independently, which takes significantly additional time that is simply entering a segment all out.

Tracking Cash Outflows

Money leaving the business to take care of tabs, pay rates, rents, and other necessities has its very own diary, the Cash Disbursements diary. This diary is the purpose of a unique section for all business money paid out to other people.

No representative likes to see cash go out the entryway, yet envision what lenders, merchants, and others would think on the off chance that they didn't get the cash they were expected. Put yourself from their point of view: Would you have the option to purchase required sup-handles if different organizations didn't pay what they owed you? No way.

You have to follow your active money similarly as cautiously as you track approaching money (see the previous area). Every passage in the Cash Disbursements journal must not just show how a lot of money was paid out yet, in addition, assign which record will be diminished in esteem in view of the money disbursal. For instance, money dispensed to take care of tabs is credited to the Cash account (which goes down in esteem) and is charged to the record from which the bill or advance is paid, for example, Accounts Payable. The charge diminishes the sum still owed in the Accounts Payable record.

In the Cash Disbursements diary, the Cash account is consistently the credit, and the charges shift contingent on the exceptional obligations to be paid

Date: The date of the exchange.

Account Debited: The name of the record charged just as any insight regarding the purpose behind the charge

Check #: The quantity of the check used to pay the obligation.

PR (post reference): Where the exchange will be posted toward the month's end. This data is filled in toward the month's end when you do the presenting on the General Ledger accounts. On the off chance that the section to be presented on the records is abridged and totaled at the base of the page, you can simply put a checkmark by the passage in the PR segment. For exchanges recorded in the General Credit or General Debit segments, you ought to show a record number for the record into which the trans-activity is posted.

General Debit: Any exchanges that don't have their own segments; these exchanges are entered independently into the records they sway.

Accounts Payable Debit: Any exchanges that are presented on the Accounts Payable record (which tracks charges due).

Salaries Debit: Debits to the Salaries business ledger, which increment the measure of compensation costs paid in a specific month.

Cash Credit: Anything that is deducted from the Cash account.

You can set up your Cash Disbursements diary with more sections on the off chance that you have accounts with visit money disbursals. For instance, in Figure 5-2, the clerk for this anecdotal organization included one segment each for Accounts Payable and Salaries since money for the two records is dispensed on various occasions during the month. As opposed to posting every dispensing in the Accounts Payable and Salaries accounts, she can simply add up to every diary section toward the month's end and add aggregates to the proper records. This methodology sure spares a great deal of time when you're working with your most dynamic record.

Manage Sales to Manage your Profit

Not all businesses include the assortment of money; numerous stores enable clients to purchase items on store credit utilizing a store Visa. (I'm not looking at purchasing with a bank-gave charge card, here; all things considered, the bank, not the store or organization making the deal, is the person who needs to stress over gathering from the client.)

Rather, store credit becomes possibly the most important factor when a client is permitted to take a store's items without paying promptly in light of the fact that he has a record that is charged month to month. This should be possible by utilizing a Visa gave by the store or some other technique the organization uses to follow credit buys by clients, for example, having the client sign a business receipt demonstrating that the sum ought to be charged to the client's record.

Deals made on store credit don't include money until the client takes care of his tab. (Interestingly, with Mastercard deals, the store gets a money installment from the card-giving bank before the client even takes care of the Visa tab.) If your organization sells on store credit, the all-out estimation of the items purchased on a specific day turns into a thing for the Accounts Receivable record, which tracks all cash due from clients.

Previously enabling clients to purchase on layaway, your organization ought to expect clients to apply for credit ahead of time with the goal that you can check their credit references

When something's sold on store credit, for the most part, the clerk drafts a receipt for the client to sign when getting the item. The receipt records the things bought and the aggregate sum due. In the wake of getting the client's signature, the receipt is followed in both the Accounts Payable record and the client's individual record.

Exchanges for deals made by store credit initially enter your books in the Sales diary. Every passage in the Sales diary must demonstrate the client's name, the receipt number, and the sum charged.

In the Sales diary, the Accounts Receivable record is charged, which increments in esteem. The clerk should likewise make sure to make a section to the client's record records on the grounds that the client has not yet paid for the thing and should be charged for it. The exchange additionally builds the estimation of the Sales account, which is credited.

Track your Purchase to Control Cash Outflow

Acquisition of items to be offered to clients sometime in the future are a key sort of non-money exchange. All organizations must have something to sell, regardless of whether they make it themselves or purchase a completed item from some other company. Organizations, as a rule, make these buys on layaway from the organization that makes the item. For this situation, the business turns into the client of another business.

Exchanges for buys purchased on layaway first enter your books in the Purchases diary. Every section in the Purchases diary must demonstrate the seller from whom the buy was made, the merchant's receipt number, and the sum charged

In the Purchases diary, the Accounts Payable record is credited, and the Purchases account is charged, which means the two records increment in esteem.

The Accounts Payable record increments in light of the fact that the organization currently owes more cash to leasers, and the Purchases account increments on the grounds that the sum spent on products to be sold up.

The Purchases diary has six segments of data:

Date: The date of the exchange.

Vendor Account Credited: The name of the merchant from whom the purchases were made.

PR (post reference): Where data about the exchange will be posted toward the month's end. This data is filled in toward the month's end when you do the presenting on the General Ledger accounts. On the off chance that the section to be presented on the records is outlined and totaled at the base of the page, you can simply put a checkmark beside the passage in the PR segment. For exchanges recorded in the General Credit or General Debit segments, you ought to show a record number for the record into which the exchange is posted.

Invoice Number: The receipt number for the buy relegated by the seller.

Purchases Debit Additions to the Purchases account.

Accounts Payable Credit: Increases to the Accounts Payable record.

Toward the month's end, the clerk can simply add up to the Purchases and Accounts Payable sections and post the sums to the relating General Ledger accounts. She can allude back to the Purchases diary for subtleties if necessary. In any case, each receipt ought to be deliberately recorded in every seller's records so that there's a running aggregate of remarkable bills for every merchant.

Posting Journal Information into Accounts

At the point when you close your books toward the month's end, you condense every one of the diaries — that is, you complete the sections and post the data to refresh every one of the records in question.

Posting diary pages is a four-advance procedure:

1. Number every diary page at the top in the event that it isn't now numbered.

2. Total any segment that is not titled General Debit or General Credit. Any exchanges recorded in the General Debit or General Credit segments should be recorded independently in General Ledger.

3. Post the passages to the General Ledger account. Every exchange in the General Credit or General Debit section must be posted independently. You simply need to present sums on General Ledger for different segments in which exchanges for increasingly dynamic records were entered in the General diary. Rundown the date and diary page number just as the measure of the charge or credit, so you can rapidly discover the passage for the first exchange in the event that you need more subtleties.

4. In the PR section of the diary, record data about where the passage is posted. On the off chance that the passage to be presented on the records is abridged and totaled at the base of the page, you can simply put a checkmark beside the section in the PR segment. For exchanges recorded in the General Credit or General Debit sections, you ought to demonstrate a record number for the record into which the exchange is posted. This procedure causes you to affirm that you've posted all passages in General Ledger.

Chapter Six

Know Your Sales

You will learn:

Ins and Out of Store Credit

How to Manage Discounts

Monitoring the Due Payments

Deal with Bad Debt

Each business wants to take in cash, and that implies you, the clerk, have a ton to do to ensure deals are appropriately followed and recorded in the books. Notwithstanding recording the business themselves, you must follow client accounts, limits offered to clients, and customer returns and stipends.

On the off chance that the organization sells items on store credit, you need to deliberately screen client accounts in Accounts Receivable, including checking whether clients pay on schedule and cautioning the business group if clients are behind on their bills and future buys using a loan should be denied. A few customers never pay, and all things considered, you should modify the books to reflect delinquency as a terrible obligation.

This part surveys the fundamental obligations that tumble to a business' accounting and bookkeeping staff for following deals, making changes in accordance with those businesses, observing client records, and cautioning the executives to slow-paying clients.

Gathering on Cash Sales

Most organizations gather some amounts of money as installments for the merchandise or services they sell. Money receipts incorporate something other than bills and coins; checks and Visas additionally are viewed as money deals with the end goal of bookkeep-ing. Actually, with electronic exchange preparing (that is the point at which a client's charge card is swiped through a machine), a store is typically made to the business' financial records that day (once in a while inside only seconds of the exchange, contingent upon the kind of framework the business sets up with the bank).

The main kind of installment that doesn't fall under the umbrella of a money payment is buys made on store credit. What's more, by store credit, I mean credit offered to clients legitimately by your business as opposed to through an outsider, for example, a bank Visa or advance. I talk progressively about this kind of offer in the segment "Selling on Credit," later in this part.

Finding the Estimation of Offers Receipts

Present-day organizations create deals slips in one of three different ways: by the money register, by the Mastercard machine, or by written by hand (out by the salesman). Whichever of these three techniques you decide to deal with your business transactions, the business receipt fills two needs:

Give the client evidence that the thing was bought on a specific day at a specific cost in your store on the off chance that he needs to trade or restore the product.

Gives the store a receipt that can be utilized sometime in the future to enter the trans-activity into the organization's books. By the day's end, the receipts likewise are utilized to demonstrate the sales enlist and guarantee that the clerk has taken in the perfect measure of money dependent on the business made.

Recording Money Exchanges in the Books

In case you're utilizing an electronic bookkeeping framework, you can enter more detail from the day's receipts and track stock sold too. The greater part of the computerized bookkeeping frameworks does incorporate the capacity to follow the clearance of stock.

Notwithstanding the data incorporated into the Cash Receipts diary, note that QuickBooks likewise gathers data about the things sold in every exchange. QuickBooks then consequently refreshes stock data, lessening the measure of stock close by when important. At the point when the stock number falls underneath the reorder number you set (see Chapter 8), QuickBooks cautions you to pass the word on to whoever is liable for requesting to arrange more stock.

On the off chance that the business receipt in Figure 9-1 was for an individual client, you'd enter their name and address in the "Offered To" field. At the base of the receipt, you can see a segment asking whether you need to print or email the receipt; you can print the receipt and offer it to the client or email it to the client if the request was made by telephone or the Internet. The base of the receipt likewise has a spot to check whether the thing ought to be charged to a Visa. (For an extra charge, QuickBooks enables you to process Mastercard receipts when sparing an individual money receipt.)

On the off chance that your organization acknowledges MasterCard, anticipate that business income should be diminished by the expenses paid to charge card organizations. For the most part, you face month-to-month charges just as expenses per exchange; notwithstanding, each organization sets up individual mastermind with its bank in regards to these expenses. Deals volume impacts the amount you pay in expenses, so when inquiring about bank administrations, make certain to contrast Visa exchange charges with locating a decent arrangement.

Selling on Credit

Numerous organizations choose to offer to clients on direct credit, which means credit offered by the business and not through a bank or charge card supplier. This methodology offers greater adaptability in the sort of terms you can offer your customers, and you don't need to pay bank expenses. In any case, it includes more work for you, the accountant, and more hazards if a client doesn't pay what the person owes.

On the off chance that you acknowledge a client's bank-gave Visa for a deal and the customer doesn't take care of the tab, you get your cash, and the bank is answerable for gathering from the client and assumes the misfortune in the event that the person doesn't pay. That is not the case in the event that you choose to offer credit to your clients straightforwardly. On the off chance that a client doesn't pay, your business assumes the misfortune.

Choosing Whether to Offer Store Credit

The choice to set up your own store credit framework relies upon what your opposition is doing. For instance, on the off chance that you run an office supply store and all other office supply stores permit store credit to make it simpler for their clients to get supplies, you likely need to offer store credit to remain aggressive.

On the off chance that you need to enable your clients to purchase on store credit, the primary thing you have to do is set up some standard procedures. You need to choose;

- How you intend to check a client's record as a consumer

- What the client's income level should be to be affirmed for credit

- How long you give the client to take care of the tab before charging interest or late expenses

The harder you make it get store credit and the stricter you make the bill-paying principles, the less possibility you have of an assuming a misfortune. Be that as it may, you may lose clients to a contender with lighter credit rules. For instance, you may require a base income level of $50,000 and make clients pay in 30 days in the event that they need to maintain a strategic distance from late expenses or intrigue charges. Your business staff reports that these guidelines are too inflexible on the grounds that your immediate rival down the road permits credit on a base income level of $30,000 and gives customers 60 days to pay before late expenses and intrigue charges. Presently you need to choose whether you need to change your credit rules to coordinate the competition. Be that as it may, on the off chance that you do bring down your credit models to coordinate your rival, you could wind up more clients who can't pay on schedule or at all since you've qualified clients for credit at lower income levels and given them more opportunity to pay. On the off chance that you extricate your capability criteria and bill-paying prerequisites, you need to painstakingly screen your client records to be certain they're not falling behind.

The key hazard you face is selling an item for which you're rarely paid. For instance, on the off chance that you enable clients 30 days to pay and cut them off from purchasing products on the off chance that their records fall over 30 days behind, at that point the most you can lose is the sum acquired over a two-month time frame (60 days). In any case, in the event that you give clients more mercy, enable them 60 days to pay, and to cut them off after installment's 30 days late, you're looked with a quarter of a year (90 days) of purchases for which you may never be paid.

Recording Store Credit Exchanges in the Books

At the point when deals are made on store credit, you need to enter explicit data into the bookkeeping framework. Notwithstanding contributing data with respect to money receipts (see "Gathering on Cash Sales" prior in this part), you update the client records to be certain every client is charged, and the cash is gathered.

Deals subtleties feed into the framework as every deal is made, so you don't need to enter the detail toward the finish of the day. The purpose of offer projects spare a ton of time; however, they can get pricey — for the most part, in any event, $400 for only one sales register is considered enough.

Regardless of whether clients don't purchase on store credit, the purpose of offer programs gives organizations a mind-boggling measure of data about their clients and what they like to purchase.

Demonstrating Out the Cash Register

To guarantee that clerks don't stash a business' money, toward the finish of every day, clerks must demonstrate out (show that they have the perfect measure of money in the register dependent on the business exchanges during the day) the measure of money, checks, and charges they took in during the day.

This procedure of demonstrating out a sales register actually begins toward the finish of the earlier day, when clerk John Doe and his administrator consent to the measure of money left in John's register cabinet. Money sitting in sales registers or money drawers is recorded as a component of the Cash on Hand record.

A senior supervisor surveys John Doe's sales register summary (created by the real register) and analyzes it to the money out a structure. On the off chance that John's completion money (the measure of money staying in the register) doesn't coordinate the money out a structure, he and the director attempt to pinpoint the misstep. On the off chance that they can't discover a mistake, they round out a money overage or money lack structure. A few organizations charge the clerk legitimately for any deficiencies, while others take the position that the clerk's terminated after a specific number of deficiencies of a specific dollar sum (say, three deficiencies of more than $10).

The senior supervisor chooses how a lot of money to leave in the money cabinet or register for the following day and stores the rest of.

He carries out this responsibility for every one of his clerks and afterward stores all the money and checks from the day in a night store box at the bank. He sends a report with subtleties of the store to the clerk, so the information makes it into the bookkeeping framework.

The clerk enters the information on the Cash Receipts structure (see Figure 9-1) if an automated bookkeeping framework is being utilized or into the Cash Receipts diary if the books are being kept physically.

Following Sales Discounts

Most businesses offer limits eventually so as to produce more deals. Limits are as a rule as a deal with 10 percent, 20 percent, or much increasingly off buys.

At the point when you offer limits to clients, it's a smart thought to follow your business limits in a different record so you can watch out for the amount you markdown deals in every month. On the off chance that you find you're losing increasingly more cash to limiting, take a gander at your evaluating structure and rivalry to discover why it's important to every now and again bring down your costs so as to make deals. You can follow rebate data effectively by utilizing the information found on a standard deals register receipt

On the off chance that you utilize a modernized bookkeeping framework, include the business markdown as a detail on the business receipt or receipt, and the framework consequently modifies the marketing projections and updates your Sales Discount account.

Recording Sales Returns and Allowances

Most stores manage deals returns all the time. It's basic for customers to return things they've bought in light of the fact that the thing is damaged, they've altered their perspectives, or for some other explanation. Establishing a no-arrival arrangement is ensured to create despondent clients, so to keep up great client relations, you ought to permit deals returns.

Deals recompenses (deals motivating force programs) are getting increasingly famous with organizations. Deals' remittances are regularly as a gift voucher. A gift voucher that is sold is really an obligation for the organization in light of the fact that the organization has gotten money, yet no product has gone out. Hence, gift voucher deals are entered into a Gift Card obligation account. At the point when a client makes a buy some time in the future utilizing the gift voucher, the Gift Card risk account is decreased by the buy sum. Checking the Gift Card risk account enables organizations to monitor what amount is yet to be sold without accepting extra money.

Tolerating deals returns can be a more convoluted procedure than tolerating deals recompenses. Normally, a business posts a lot of decides for restores that may include:

Returns might be permitted inside 30 days of procurement.

You should have a receipt to restore a thing.

If you return a thing without a receipt, you can get just store credit.

You can set up whatever rules you need for returns. Much of the time, you ought to require an administrator's endorsement on returns.

Additionally, be certain your staff gives close consideration to how the client initially paid for the thing being returned. You absolutely would prefer not to give client money in the event that she paid on store credit — that is simply giving over your cash! After an arrival's affirmed, the clerk either restores the sum paid with money or Visa. Clients who purchased the things on store credit don't recover any cash. That is on the grounds that they didn't pay anything when they bought the thing, yet expected to be charged later. Rather, a structure is rounded out with the goal that the sum of the first buy can be subtracted from the client's store credit account

Checking Accounts Receivable

Ensuring clients take care of their tabs is an urgent obligation of the accountant. Prior to conveying the month-to-month charges, you ought to set up an Aging Summary Report that rundowns all clients who owe cash to the organization and how old every obligation is. On the off chance that you keep the books physically, you gather the necessary data from every client account. On the off chance that you keep the books in a modernized bookkeeping framework, you can create this report naturally. In any case, your Aging Summary Report should seem to be like this model report from a pastry kitchen:

The Aging Summary rapidly reveals to you, which clients are behind in their bills. On account of this model, clients are cut off from future buys when their installments are over 60 days late, so J. Doe and M. Man aren't ready to purchase on store credit until their bills are forked over the required funds.

Give a duplicate of your Aging Summary to the team lead so he can alarm staff to issue clients. He can likewise organize suitable assortments methods. Every business sets up its own assortments procedure, yet for the most part, it begins with a telephone call, trailed by letters, and perhaps even lawful activity, if essential.

Tolerating Your Losses

You may experience a circumstance wherein your business never gets paid by a client, considerably after a forceful assortment process. For this situation, you must choose the option to discount the buy as a terrible obligation and acknowledge the misfortune.

Most organizations survey their Aging Reports each six to a year and choose which records should be discounted as a terrible obligation. Records discounted are followed in a General Ledger account called Bad Debt. The Bad Debt account shows up as a business ledger on the income statement. At the point when you discount a client's record as a terrible obligation, the Bad Debt account increments, and the Accounts Receivable record diminishes.

Chapter Seven

Depreciating Assets

You will learn:

Why you Add Deprecations in Accounts

Looking at Depreciation Tax Benefits

Entering Depreciation Expenses in Accounts

Organizations use hardware, goods, and vehicles that last over a year. Any benefit that has a life expectancy of over a year is called a fixed resource. They may last longer than different resources, yet even fixed resources, in the end, get old and need supplanting.

What's more, in light of the fact that your business should coordinate its costs with its income, you would prefer not to discount the full cost of a fixed resource in one year. All things considered, you'll unquestionably be utilizing the benefit for over one year.

Envision how awful your salary articulation would look in the event that you discounted the expense of a $100,000 bit of hardware in only one year? It would sure look as though your business wasn't progressing nicely. Envision the effect on a private company — $100,000 could gobble up its whole benefit or possibly put it in the situation of detailing a misfortune.

Rather than discounting everything of a fixed resource in one year, you utilize a bookkeeping technique canceled devaluation to compose the advantage as it gets spent. In this section, I acquaint you with the different ways you can deteriorate your benefits and disclose how to figure devaluation, how devaluation impacts both the pay articulation and your expense bill, and how to record devaluation in your books.

What is Depreciation?

You may consider devaluation something that happens to your vehicle as it loses esteem. Truth be told, most new vehicles devalue 20 to 30 percent or much more when you drive them off the parcel. Be that as it may, when you're discussing account-ing, the meaning of devaluation is somewhat unique.

Basically, bookkeepers use devaluation as an approach to apportion the expenses of a fixed resource over the period in which the benefit is useable to the business. You, the clerk, record the full exchange when the benefit is purchased, yet the estimation of the advantage is step by step decreased by subtracting a bit of that incentive as a devaluation cost every year. Devaluation costs don't include the

trade of money. They're exclusively accomplished for bookkeeping purposes. Most organizations enter deterioration costs into the books once every year just before setting up their yearly reports; however, others ascertain devaluation costs month-to-month or quarterly.

One key motivation to discount resources is to bring down your assessment bill, so the IRS engages in deterioration, as well. As an entrepreneur, you can't discount the expense of every single significant buy in one year. Rather the IRS has exacting principles about how you can discount resources as duty deductible costs. I talk increasingly about the IRS's principles in the segment, "Handling Taxes and Depreciation," later in this section.

Identifying the Assets on the Basis of Depreciation

Organizations don't devalue all advantages. Minimal effort things or things that aren't relied upon to last over one year are recorded in business ledgers instead of benefit accounts. For instance, office supplies are cost things and not deteriorated; however, that office copier, which you'll use for over one year, is recorded in the books as a fixed resource and devalued every year.

Life expectancy isn't the central factor for deterioration, be that as it may. A few resources that last numerous years are never devalued. One genuine model island; you can generally utilize land, so its worth never devalue. You additionally can't depreciate any property that you rent or lease, however in the event that you make enhancements to rented property; you can devalue the expense of those upgrades. All things considered, you discount the rent or lease as a cost thing and deteriorate the rent upgrades over their evaluated helpful life.

You can't devalue any things that you use outside your business, for example, your own vehicle or home PC, yet on the off chance that you utilize these benefits for both personal necessities and business needs, you can deteriorate a part of them dependent on the level of time or other estimation that demonstrates the amount you utilize the vehicle or PC for business. For instance, the segment of a vehicle that can be deteriorated depends on the miles driven for business versus the miles driven for individual use. On the off chance that you drive your vehicle an aggregate of 12,000 miles in a year and have records demonstrating that 6,000 of those miles were for business, you can devalue 50 percent of the expense of the vehicle. That rate is apportioned over the foreseen valuable existence of the vehicle

Another cause of a deterioration of a double utilization resource is a room in your home assigned only for your business. You might have the option to depreciate-ate a bit of your home's cost as a major aspect of your operational expense. The sum you can devalue depends on the segment of your home utilized for business.

Methods used for Depreciation

While computing devaluation of your advantages every year, you have a decision of four strategies: Straight-Line, Sum-of-Years-Digits, Double-Declining Balance, and Units of Production. In this segment, I clarify these strategies just as the upsides and downsides of utilizing everyone.

Straight-Line

While deteriorating resources utilizing the Straight-Line technique, you spread the expense of the benefit equally over the number of years the advantage will be utilized. Straight-Line is the most well-known technique utilized for deterioration of advantages, and it's likewise the least demanding one to utilize. Another bit of leeway of this technique is that you can utilize it for both bookkeeping purposes and duty purposes. (On the off chance that you utilize any of different strategies, you need to keep separate deterioration records — one for your money related reports and one for the expense man.

The equation for computing Straight-Line deterioration is:

(Cost of fixed resource − Salvage) Estimated valuable life = Annual devaluation cost

For the truck in this model, the cost premise is $25,000, the rescue esteem is

$5,000, and I'm utilizing the IRS gauge of the helpful existence of five years. With these figures, the count for finding the yearly deterioration cost of this truck dependent on the Straight-Line devaluation strategy is:

($25,000 − $5,000) 5 = $4,000

Every year, the business' Income Statement ought to incorporate $4,000 as a depreciation cost for this truck. You add this $4,000 devaluation cost to the collected deterioration represents the truck. This collected depreciation account appears underneath the truck's unique incentive on the Balance Sheet. You subtract the gathered deterioration from the estimation of the truck to show net resource esteem, which is worth staying on the truck.

Total of-Years-Digits

On the off chance that you think your advantage loses a more noteworthy segment of its valuable life in the early years, you can accelerate its deterioration by utilizing the Sum-of-Years-Digits (SYD) technique. This strategy enables you to discount higher devaluation costs in the previous long periods of helpful life and lower deterioration in later years. At the point when you use Sum-of-

Years-Digits, you expect that the fixed resource will be utilized less in later years

One major impediment of discounting resources rapidly is that the higher depreciation cost brings down your business's net gain.

Units of Production

The Units of Production (UOP) technique for deterioration functions admirably principally in an assembling situation since it computes devaluation dependent on the number of units delivered in a year. Organizations whose apparatus utilization differs extraordinarily every year relying upon the market and the number of units required available to be purchased utilize this deterioration strategy.

Chapter Eight

Treatment of Interest as Income or Expenses

You will learn:

Treating Different Types of Finances

Expense vs. Income

Measuring Interests

Barely any organizations can make significant buys without taking out credits regardless of whether advances are for vehicles, structures, or different business needs.

Organizations must compensation premium, a level of the sum lent, to whoever credits them the cash.

A few organizations credit their own cash and get premium installments as pay. Actually, an investment account can be viewed as a sort of advance on the grounds that by putting your cash in the record, you're allowing the bank the chance to credit that cash to other people. So the bank pays you for the utilization of your cash by paying the premium, which is a kind of pay for your organization.

This part surveys various kinds of credits and how to figure and record intrigue costs for each sort. Also, I examine how you ascertain and record intrigue salary in your business' books.

Self-Multiplying Dividends

Self-multiplying dividends are registered on both the head and any premium earned. You should figure the premium every year and add it to the parity before you can compute the following year's advantage installment, which will be founded on both the head and premium earned.

Here's the manner by which you would ascertain self-multiplying dividends:

Head x premium rate = enthusiasm for year one (Principal + premium earned) x loan fee = enthusiasm for year two (Principal + premium earned) x financing cost = enthusiasm for year three

You rehash this figuring for all long stretches of the store or credit. The one exception could be with an advance. On the off chance that you pay the complete enthusiasm due every month or year (contingent upon when your installments are expected), there would be no enthusiasm for the compound.

You can see that you'd win an extra $27.27 during the initial three years of that store if the intrigue is exacerbated. When working with a lot bigger aggregates of higher financing costs for longer timeframes, accumulating funds can have a major effect on the amount you procure or the amount you pay on credit.

In a perfect world, you need to discover a bank account, testament store, or other savings instruments that acquire accruing funds. Be that as it may, on the off chance that you need to obtain cash, search for a straightforward premium credit.

Additionally, not all records that win progressive accrual are made similarly. Watch cautiously to perceive how every now and again, the intrigue is intensified. The former model shows a sort of record for which intrigue is aggravated every year. In any case, on the off chance that you discover a record where a premium is exacerbated month-to-month, the premium you procure will be considerably higher. Month to month intensifying implies that between EST earned will be determined every month and added to the guideline every prior month ascertaining the following month's advantage, which brings about significantly more enthusiasm than a bank that mixes premium just once per year.

Treatment of Interest Income

The pay that your business procures from its bank accounts, endorsements of stores, or other speculation vehicles is called premium pay. As the accountant, you're infrequently required to compute intrigue salary utilizing the basic intrigue or exacerbated intrigue recipes portrayed in the prior areas of this section. Much of the time, the budgetary establishment sends you a month to month, quarterly, or yearly articulation that has a different detail announcing premium earned.

At the point when you get your month-to-month proclamation, you at that point accommodate the books. Compromise is a procedure wherein you demonstrate out whether the sum the bank says you have in your record is equivalent to what you think you have in your record.

Chapter Nine

Closing Journals

You will learn:

>*Checking the Authenticity of Journals*

>*Posting Adjustments in a Ledger*

>*Examining Journals via a Computerized System*

In the event that you utilize a modernized bookkeeping framework to do your books, you don't have to finish off your diaries, yet you can, at present, run a progression of reports to confirm that all the data in the PC bookkeeping framework matches what you have on paper. I talk about how to do that quickly in this part.

This section centers principally on how to demonstrate your diaries and close them toward the finish of a bookkeeping period. (Section 14 sees this procedure for money diaries specifically, in case you're intrigued.) You additionally discover how to post all redresses and alterations, to General Ledger after you make them in the fitting diary

Preparing to Close: Checking for Accuracy and Tallying Things Up

As you get ready to close the books, you first need to add up to what is in your journals, which is called abridging the diaries. During the procedure, it's a smart thought to search for unmitigated mistakes and be certain that the passages precisely mirror the exchanges during the bookkeeping time frame.

Indeed, even the littlest mistake in a diary can cause a great deal of disappointment when you attempt to run a preliminary balance and close out your books, so it's ideal to do a thorough scan for blunders as you close out every diary for the month. It's a lot simpler to discover a mistake now in the end procedure than to attempt to follow it back through the entirety of your different records.

Focusing on Starting Exchange Subtleties

Do a speedy check to be certain the exchange subtleties in your diaries are accurate. Section 14 discloses to you how to do this sort of check with the money diaries, yet when you adhere to the guidelines of gathering bookkeeping, not all exchanges include money. In accumulation bookkeeping, noncash exchanges can incorporate customer buys made on store credit (which you track in the Accounts Receivable diary) and bills you will pay later on (which you track in the Accounts Payable diary). You may likewise have made different diaries to follow exchanges in your most dynamic records, and you presumably additionally keep insights concerning deals in the Sales diary and finance in the Payroll diary.

In the Payroll diary, ensure that all payrolls for the month have been included with all the best possible insights concerning compensations, compensation, and duties. Additionally, check that you've recorded all business assesses that should be paid. These charges incorporate the business' segment of Medicare and Social Security just as joblessness charges.

Outlining Diary Passages

The initial phase in checking for exactness in your diaries is condensing them, which is essentially totaling every one of the sections in the diary. This rundown procedure gives you aggregates for the records being followed by every diary. For instance, outlining the Accounts Receivable diary gives you an amazing aggregate of all exchanges for that period that included client credit accounts.

The Accounts Receivable diary incorporates exchanges from the Sales diary (where the client buys on store credit initially show up) and the Cash Receipts diary (where clients' installments toward their store credit accounts initially show up) just as any credit updates for client returns.

At the point when you condense the Accounts Receivable journal, you get an end balance, a balance that shows the aggregate of all money related movement recorded in that diary.

Every exchange in the diary ought to have a reference number by it, which discloses to you where the detail for that exchange initially shows up in the books. You may need to audit this data later when you're demonstrating out the books. At the point when you check for blunders in the diary, you may need to audit the first source data used to enter a few exchanges so as to twofold watch that section's exactness.

Notwithstanding the Accounts Receivable diary, you likewise have individual journal pages for every client; these pages detail every client's buys on store credit and any installments made toward those buys. Toward the finish of a bookkeeping period, set up a maturing rundown itemizing all remarkable client accounts. This report gives you what cash is expected from customers and to what extent it has been expected.

On the off chance that you discover a distinction between the data in your diary and your maturing rundown, survey your client account exchanges to discover the issue.

A blunder might be the aftereffect of

Recording a business exchange without recording the subtleties of that trans-activity in the client's record.

Recording a buy legitimately into the client's record without add the buy add up to the Accounts Receivable diary.

Recording a client's installment in the client's record without recording the money receipt in the Accounts Receivable diary.

Recording a client's installment in the Accounts Receivable diary without recording the money receipt in the client's record.

The aggregate of exceptional bills on the Accounts Payable Aging Summary should coordinate the all-out appeared on the Accounts Payable diary synopsis for the bookkeeping time frame. On the off chance that your match, you're prepared for a preliminary balance. In the event that they don't, you should make sense of purpose behind the distinction before finishing off the Accounts Payable diary.

Right, any issues you find before finishing off the diary. In the event that you realize that you might be working with off base information, you would prefer not to attempt to do a preliminary balance since you realize that balance will be documented with mistakes, and you won't have the option to produce exact money related reports. Additionally, in the event that you realize blunders exist, it resembles the books won't balance in any case, so it's only a squandered exercise to do a preliminary balance.

Examining Outline Results

You might be thinking about how you can discover issues in your records by simply investigating a page in a diary. All things considered that aptitude accompanies understanding and practice. As you outline your diaries every month, you'll become acquainted with the normal degree of exchanges and the sorts of exchange that happen a seemingly endless amount of time after a month. On the off chance that you don't see an exchange that you hope to discover, set aside the effort to investigate the exchange to discover why it's absent.

It's conceivable that the exchange didn't occur, but on the other hand, it's conceivable that somebody neglected to record it.

For instance, assume that when abridging the Payroll diary, you see that the finance for the fifteenth of the month appears lower than typical. As you check your subtleties for that finance, you find that the sum paid to hourly workers was recorded; however, somebody didn't record the sum paid to salaried representatives. For that specific finance, the finance organization experienced a PC issue in the wake of running a few checks and therefore sent the last report on two separate pages. The individual who recorded the finance numbers didn't understand there was a different page for salaried workers, so the last numbers went into the books that didn't mirror everything paid to representatives.

As you close the books every month, you'll get a thought of the numbers you can expect for each sort of diary. Sooner or later, you'll have the option to select issues just by checking a page — no point by point inquire about required!

Getting Ready for Income

The procedure you experience every month as you get ready to close your books causes you to plan for future income. Evaluating the Accounts Receivable and Accounts Payable Aging Summaries reveals to you what extra money you can anticipate from clients during the following hardly any months and how a lot of money you'll require so as to take care of tabs for the following barely any months.

In the event that you see that your Accounts Payable Aging Summary shows that an ever-increasing number of bills are slipping into past-due status, you may need to discover another hotspot for money, for example, a credit line from the bank. For instance, the Accounts Payable Aging Summary uncovers that three key sellers — Helen's Paper Goods, Henry's Bakery Supplies, and Plates Unlimited — haven't been paid on schedule. Late installments can hurt your business' working association with merchants; they may decline to convey merchandise except if money is paid forthright. What's more, on the off chance that you can't get the crude materials you need, you may experience difficulty dispatching client arranges on schedule. The exercise here is to act rapidly and figure out how to improve income before your merchants cut you off.

Presenting on the General Ledger

A significant piece of shutting your books is presenting on General Ledger, any rectifications or modifications you find as you close the diaries. This kind of posting comprises of a basic section that abridges any progressions you found.

For instance, assume you locate that a client buy was recorded legitimately in the client's record; however, not in the Accounts Receivable diary. You need to look into how that exchange was initially recorded.

On the off chance that you discover this kind of blunder, the Sales exchange record for that date of the offer isn't precise, which implies that somebody skirted your standard accounting process when recording the deal. You might need to investigate that piece of the issue, too, in light of the fact that there might be something other than a chronicle issue behind this occurrence. Somebody in your organization might be enabling clients to take an item, intentionally not recording the deal properly in your books, and taking the cash. It's likewise conceivable that a salesman recorded a deal for a client that never occurred. On the off chance that that is the situation and you charge the client, he would probably scrutinize the bill, and you'd get some answers concerning the issue by then.

The way toward demonstrating out your diaries, or some other piece of your accounting records, is a decent chance to audit your inside controls also. As you discover blunders during the way toward demonstrating out the books, watch out for ones (most likely comparable blunders that show up habitually) that may show more serious issues than simply accounting missteps. Rehash mistakes may require extra staff preparing to be certain your accounting rules are being pursued perfectly. Or on the other hand, such blunders might be proof that somebody in the organization is intentionally recording bogus data. Whatever the clarification, you have to make the restorative move. (I spread inner controls top to bottom in Chapter 7.)

Looking at Computerized Journal Records

Despite the fact that you don't need to finish off diary pages in the event that you keep your books utilizing an electronic bookkeeping framework, running a spot-check (at any rate) of what you have in your paper records versus what you have on your PC is a keen move. Basically, run a progression of reports utilizing your computerized bookkeeping framework and afterward check to be certain that those PC records coordinate what you have in your documents.

Chapter Ten

Adjusting the Books

You will learn:

How to Adjust Books

Understanding the Key Areas

Tallying Stock and Understanding Costs

During a bookkeeping period, your accounting obligations center on your business' everyday exchanges. At the point when it comes time to report those exchanges in fiscal reports, you should make a few changes in accordance with your books. Your monetary reports should show your organization's money related wellbeing, so your books must mirror any noteworthy change in the estimation of your advantages, regardless of whether that change doesn't include the trading of money.

On the off chance that you use money premise bookkeeping, these alterations aren't important on the grounds that you possibly record exchanges when money changes hands.

This part surveys the sorts of alterations you have to make to the books before setting up the budget summaries, including figuring resource devaluation, splitting prepaid costs, refreshing stock numbers, managing terrible obligation, and perceiving pay rates and wages not yet paid. You additionally discover how to include and erase accounts.

Modifying All the Right Areas

Much subsequent to testing your books utilizing the preliminary balance process that I clarify in Chapter 16, despite everything, you have to make a few changes before you're ready to plan precise money related reports with the data you have. These changes don't include the trading of money yet rather include perceiving the utilization of benefits, loss of advantages, or future resource commitments that aren't reflected in everyday accounting exercises.

Deteriorating Resources

The highest noncash cost for most organizations is deterioration. Deterioration is a bookkeeping exercise that is significant for each business to attempt since it mirrors the utilization and maturing of advantages. More seasoned resources need more support and fix and furthermore should be supplanted in the long run. As the deterioration of advantage increments and the estimation of the benefit lessens, the requirement for more upkeep or substitution gets obvious.

The opportunity to really make this change in accordance with the books is the point at which you close the books for a bookkeeping period. (A few organizations record devaluation costs each month to all the more precisely coordinate month-to-month costs with month-to-month incomes, however, most entrepreneurs just stress over deterioration alterations on a yearly premise, when they set up their yearly fiscal reports.)

Deterioration doesn't include the utilization of money. By amassing devaluation costs on an advantage, you're lessening the estimation of the benefit as appeared on the balance sheet (see Chapter 18 for the lowdown on balance sheets).

For the most part, you figure devaluation for bookkeeping purposes utilizing the straight-line devaluation strategy. This strategy is utilized to compute and add up the amount to be deteriorated that will be equivalent every year, dependent on the foreseen valuable existence of the advantage. For instance, assume your organization buys a vehicle for business purposes that expenses $25,000. You envision that the vehicle will have a helpful life expectancy of five years and will be worth $5,000 following five years. Utilizing the straight-line deterioration strategy, you subtract $5,000 from the all-out vehicle cost of $25,000 to discover the estimation of the vehicle during its five-year helpful life expectancy ($20,000). At that point, you partition $20,000 by 5 to discover your deterioration cost for the vehicle ($4,000 every year).

You can accelerate deterioration in the event that you accept that the benefit won't be utilized equally over its life expectancy — to be specific, that the advantage will be utilized all the more intensely in the long early stretches of proprietorship.

On the off chance that you utilize a mechanized bookkeeping framework rather than keeping your books physically, you might possibly need to make this modification toward the finish of a bookkeeping period. In the event that your framework is set up with a benefit the board highlight, devaluation is naturally determined, and you don't need to stress over it. Check with your bookkeeper (the individual in question is the person who might set up the benefit the executives include) before ascertaining and recording devaluation costs.

Dispensing Prepaid Costs

Most organizations need to pay certain costs toward the start of the year despite the fact that they will profit by that cost consistently. Protection is a prime case of this kind of cost. Most insurance agencies expect you to pay the premium every year toward the beginning of the year despite the fact that the estimation of that protection secures the organization consistently.

For instance, assume your organization's yearly vehicle protection premium is

$1,200. You pay that premium in January so as to keep up protection inclusion consistently. Demonstrating the full money cost of your protection when you set up your January budgetary reports would enormously lessen any benefit that month and exacerbate your monetary outcomes look than the really are. That is nothing more than trouble.

This section builds protection costs on the income statement and diminishes the advantage of Prepaid Expenses on the balance sheet. No money changes submit this section since money was spread out when the protection bill was paid, and the benefit account Prepaid Expenses was expanded in an incentive at the time the money was paid.

Tallying Stock

Stock is a balance sheet resource that should be balanced toward the finish of a bookkeeping period. During the bookkeeping time frame, your organization purchases inventory and records those buys in a Purchases account without demonstrating any change to stock. At the point when the items are sold, you record the deals in the Sales account, however, don't make any change in accordance with the estimation of the inventory. Rather, you alter the stock an incentive toward the finish of the bookkeeping time frame in light of the fact that modifying with each buys and a deal would be far and away also tedious.

The means for making legitimate changes in accordance with stock in your books are as per the following:

1. Determine the stock remaining.

    Notwithstanding ascertaining consummation stock utilizing the buys and deals numbers in the books, you ought to likewise do a physical tally of stock to be certain that what's on the racks coordinates what's in the books.

2. Set an incentive for that stock.

    The benefit of consummation stock differs, relying upon the strategy your organization has decided to use for esteeming stock.

3. Adjust the number of pieces staying in stock in the Inventory Account and modify the estimation of that record dependent on the data gathered in Steps 1 and 2.

In the event that you track stock utilizing your mechanized bookkeeping framework, the framework makes changes in accordance with stock as you record deals. Toward the finish of the recording period, the estimation of your organization's consummation stock ought to be balanced in the books as of now. Despite the fact that the work's now accomplished for you, you should, at present, do a physical tally of the stock to be certain that your PC records coordinate the physical stock toward the finish of the bookkeeping time frame.

Testing Out an Adjusted Trial Balance

You track all the modifying sections on a worksheet. You possibly need to do this worksheet in case you're doing your books physically. It's a bit much in case you're utilizing an electronic bookkeeping framework.

The key contrast in the worksheet for the Adjusted Trial Balance is that four extra sections must be added to the worksheet for an aggregate of 11 segments. Sections incorporate

Section 1: Account titles.

Sections 2 and 3: Unadjusted Trial Balance. The preliminary balance before the modifications are made with Column 2 for charges and Column 3 for credits.

Sections 4 and 5: Adjustments. All acclimations to the preliminary balance are recorded in Column 4 for charges and Column 5 for credits.

Sections 6 and 7: Adjusted Trial Balance. Another preliminary balance is determined that incorporates every one of the modifications. Be certain that the credits equivalent the charges when you complete that new Trial Balance. On the off chance that they don't, discover any mistakes before adding passages to the balance sheet and income statement segments.

Segments 8 and 9: the Balance sheet. Section 8 incorporates all the Balance Sheet accounts that have a charge balance, and Column 9 incorporates all the Balance Sheet accounts with a credit balance.

Sections 10 and 11: the Income statement. Segment 10 incorporates all the Income Statement accounts with a charge Balance, and Column 11 incorporates all the Income Statement accounts with a credit balance.

At the point when you're sure that every one of the records is in balance, present your alterations on General Ledger with the goal that every one of the balances in General Ledger incorporates the changing sections. With the modifications, General Ledger will coordinate the budget summaries you get ready.

Changing Your Chart of Accounts

After you finish your General Ledger for the year, you might need to make changes to your Chart of Accounts, which records every one of the records in your bookkeeping framework. You may need to include accounts on the off chance that you think you need extra ones or erase accounts in the event that you figure they will never again be required.

You should just erase accounts from your graph of records toward the year's end. On the off chance that you erase a record in the year, your yearly fiscal reports won't mirror the exercises in that record before its cancellation. So regardless of whether you choose a part of the way during that time to never again utilize a record, you should leave it on the books until the year's end, and afterward erase it.

You can add records to your Chart of Accounts consistently, however in the event that you choose to include a record in the year so as to all the more intently track certain advantages, liabilities, incomes, or costs; you may need to modify some related sections.

Assume you start the year out following paper costs in the Office Supplies Expenses account, however paper utilization and its cost continue expanding, so you choose to follow the cost in a different record starting in July.

Initially, you include the new record, Paper Expenses, to your Chart of Accounts. At that point, you set up a modifying section to move all the paper costs that were recorded in the Office Supplies Expenses record to the Paper Expenses account. In light of a legitimate concern for space and to abstain from exhausting you, the modifying passage beneath is a shortened one.

Moving Past the Catchall Miscellaneous Expenses Account

At the point when new records are added to the Chart of Accounts, the record most normally balanced is the Miscellaneous Expenses account. Much of the time, you may hope to cause a cost just a couple of times during the year, subsequently making it superfluous to make another record explicitly for that cost. In any case, sooner or later, you find that your "uncommon" cost is including, and you'd be in an ideal situation with an assigned record, implying that it's a great opportunity to make some modifying passages to move costs out of the Miscellaneous Expenses account.

For instance, assume you think you'll just need to lease a vehicle for the business one time before you purchase another vehicle, so you enter the rental expense in the books as a Miscellaneous Expense. In any case, subsequent to leasing vehicles multiple times, you choose to begin a Rental Expense account mid-year. At the point when you add the Rental Expense record to your Chart of Accounts, you have to utilize a changing passage to move any costs acquired and recorded in the Miscellaneous Expense account before the formation of the new record.

Chapter Eleven

Understanding the Concept of a Balance Sheet

You will learn:

    The Essentials of a Balance Sheet

    Choosing the Right Format

    Drawing the Conclusion from the Balance Sheet

This section clarifies the key elements of a balance sheet and discloses to you how to pull them all together. You likewise discover how to utilize some systematic devices considered proportions to perceive how well your business is getting along.

What Is a Balance Sheet?

Essentially, making a balance sheet resembles snapping a photo of the money related parts of your business.

The organization name and consummation date for the bookkeeping time frame being accounted for show up at the highest point of the balance sheet. The remainder of the report abridges

The organization's benefits, which incorporate everything the organization claims so as to remain in the business.

The organization's obligations, which incorporate any extraordinary bills and advances that must be paid.

The proprietor's value, which is essentially how much the organization proprietors have put resources into the business.

Resources, liabilities, and value likely solid natural — they're the key elements that show whether your books are in balance. In the event that your liabilities in addition to value equivalent resources, your books are in balance.

You can discover the majority of the data you have to set up a balance sheet on your preliminary balance worksheet, the subtleties of which are drawn from your last balanced preliminary balance.

Partitioning and Posting your Advantages

The initial segment of the balance sheet is the Assets segment. The initial phase in building up this area is isolating your advantages into two classifications: current resources and long haul resources.

Current Resources

Current resources are things your organization possesses that you can without much of a stretch convert to money and hope to use in the following a year to take care of your tabs and your representatives. Current resources incorporate money, Accounts Receivable (cash due from clients), attractive protections (counting stocks, securities, and different sorts of protections), and stock.

At the point when you consider money to be the principal detail on a balance sheet, that record incorporates what you have close by in the register and what you have in the bank, including financial records, investment accounts, currency showcase records, and authentications of the store. Much of the time, you essentially list every one of these records as one thing, Cash, on the balance sheet.

Long Haul Resources

Long haul resources are things your organization possesses that you hope to have for over a year. Long haul resources incorporate land, structures, gear, furniture, vehicles, and whatever else that you hope to have for longer than a year.

Most organizations have more things in the long haul resources segment of a balance sheet than the couple of long haul resources I appear here for the anecdotal organization.

For instance, an assembling organization that has plenty of devices passes on, or molds made explicitly for its assembling procedures would have a detail called Tools, Dies, and Molds in the long haul resources area of the balance sheet.

So also, if your organization possesses at least one structure, you ought to have a detail named Land and Buildings. Also, in the event that you rent a structure with a choice to buy it at some later date, that promoted rent is viewed as a long haul resource and recorded on the balance sheet as Capitalized Lease.

A few organizations rent their business space and afterward spend loads of cash setting it up. For instance, a café may lease a huge space and afterward outfit it as per an ideal subject. Cash spent on repairing the space turns into a long haul resource called Leasehold Improvements and is recorded on the balance sheet in the long haul resources area.

All that I've referenced so far in this segment — land, structures, promoted leases, leasehold enhancements, etc. — is an unmistakable resource. These are things that you can really contact or hold. Another kind of long haul resource is the immaterial resource. Elusive resources aren't physical objects; the normal tests are licenses, copyrights, and trademarks (which are all conceded by the legislature).

Patents give organizations the privilege to overwhelm the business sectors for licensed items. At the point when patent lapses (14 to 20 years relying upon the kind of patent), contenders can enter the commercial center for the item that was licensed, and the challenge brings down the cost to consumers. For instance, pharmaceutical organizations patent all their new medications and in this way, are ensured as the sole suppliers of those medications. At the point when your primary care physician recommends a brand-name medicate, you're getting a licensed item. Conventional drugs are items whose licenses have run out, implying that any pharmaceutical organization can create and sell its own rendition of a similar item.

Copyrights ensure unique works, including books, magazines, articles, papers, network shows, films, music, verse, and plays, from being duplicated by anybody other than their makers. For instance, this book is copyrighted, so nobody can make a duplicate of any of its substance without the consent of the distributor, Wiley Publishing, Inc.

Trademarks give organizations responsibility for words, expressions, images, or plans. For instance, look at this present book's spread to see the enrolled trademark, For Dummies, for this brand. Trademarks can keep going perpetually up to an organization, keeps on utilizing the trademark, and document the correct administrative work occasionally.

So as to appear in budget summaries that their qualities are being spent, all long haul resources are either devalued or amortized. Unmistakable resources are deteriorated; see Chapter 12 for subtleties on the best way to devalue. Immaterial resources, for example, licenses and copyrights, are amortized (amortization is fundamentally the same as devaluation). Every immaterial resource has a life expectancy depends on the number of years the administration allows the rights for it. Subsequent to setting an underlying incentive for the elusive resource, an organization at that point isolates that incentive by the number of years it has government security, and the subsequent sum is then discounted every year as an Amortization Expense, which is appeared on the pay explanation.

You can locate the absolute amortization or devaluation costs that have been discounted during the life of the benefit on the Balance Sheet in detail called Accumulated Depreciation or Accumulated Amortization, whichever is appropriate for the sort of advantage.

Recognizing your Obligations

The Liabilities segment of the balance sheet comes after the Assets area (see the "Partitioning and posting your benefits" segment) and shows all the cash that your business owes to other people, including banks, merchants, contractual workers, budgetary organizations, or people. Like resources, you isolate your liabilities into two classifications on the balance sheet:

Current liabilities: All bills and obligations you intend to pay inside the following year. Records showing up in this segment incorporate

Accounts Payable (charges because of sellers, contractual workers, and others), Credit Card Payable, and the present segment of a long haul obligation (for instance, on the off chance that you have a mortgage on your store, the installments due in the following a year show up in the Current Liabilities area).

Long-term liabilities: All obligations you owe to moneylenders that will be paid over a period longer than a year. Home loans Payable, Loans Payable, and Bonds Payable are normal accounts in the long haul liabilities segment of the balance sheet.

Most organizations attempt to limit their present liabilities in light of the fact that the financing costs on transient advances, for example, MasterCard, are normally a lot higher than those on advances with longer terms. As you deal with your organization's liabilities, you ought to consistently search for approaches to limit your advantage installments by look for longer-term advances with lower financing costs than you can jump on a Visa or momentary credit.

Taking Help from the Balance Sheet

With a total balance sheet in your grasp, you can investigate the numbers through a progression of proportion tests to check your money status and track your obligation. Since these are the sorts of tests monetary organizations and potential speculators use to decide if to credit cash to or put resources into your organization, it's a smart thought to run these tests yourself before looking for advances or financial specialists. Eventually, the proportion of tests spread in this area can enable you to prevent whether your organization is in a solid money position or not.

Testing your Money

At the point when you approach a bank or other money-related organization for an advance, you can anticipate that the moneylender should utilize one of two proportions to test your income: the present proportion and the basic analysis proportion (otherwise called the brisk proportion).

Current Proportion

Loan specialists typically search for momentum proportions of 1.2 to 2, so any money related organization would consider a flow proportion of 2.36 a decent sign. A present proportion under 1 is viewed as a peril sign since it demonstrates the organization needs more money to take care of its present tabs.

A present proportion over 2.0 may show that your organization isn't contributing its advantages well and might have the option to utilize its present resources. For instance, if your organization is holding a great deal of money, you might need to put that cash in some long haul resources, for example, extra hardware that you have to help develop the business.

Basic Analysis (brisk) Proportion

The basic analysis proportion just uses the money related figures in your organization's Cash account, Accounts Receivable, and Marketable Securities. In spite of the fact that it's similar to the present proportion in that it analyzes current resources and liabilities, the basic analysis proportion is a stricter trial of your organization's capacity to take care of tabs. The advantages some portion of this figurine doesn't consider in light of the fact that it can't generally be changed over to money as fast as other current resources and on the grounds that, in a moderate market, selling your stock may take some time.

Numerous moneylenders lean toward the analysis proportion while deciding if to give you credit as a result of its severity.

Surveying your Obligation

Before you even think about whether to assume the extra obligation, you ought to consistently look at your obligation condition. One regular proportion that you can use to evaluate your organization's obligation position is the obligation to value proportion. This proportion looks at what your business owes to what your business possesses.

Creating Balance Sheets Electronically

In the event that you utilize a modernized bookkeeping framework, you can exploit its report capacity to produce your balance sheets consequently. These balance sheets give you speedy previews of the organization's monetary position yet may require modifications before you set up your budgetary reports for outside use.

One key change you're probably going to make includes the estimation of your stock. Most modernized bookkeeping frameworks utilize the averaging technique to esteem stock. This strategy adds up to all the stock acquired and afterward computes a normal cost for the stock for more data on stock valuation. In any case, your bookkeeper may prescribe an alternate valuation technique that works better for your business.

Chapter Twelve

Making an Income Statement

You will learn:

Sorting the Income Statement

Preparing an Income Statement

Analyzing the Income Statement

Calculate Profitability

The income statement is considered as one significant money related report apparatus; you'd never know without a doubt whether your business made a benefit. This device is called the income statement, and most organizations set them up on a month-to-month premise just as quarterly and every year so as to get intermittent pictures of how well the business is getting along monetarily.

Breaking down the income statement and the subtleties behind it can uncover heaps of valuable data to assist you with settling on choices for improving your benefits and business by and large. This section covers the pieces of an income statement, how you created one, and instances of how you can utilize it to settle on business choices.

What Is an Income Statement?

Did your business profit? You can discover the appropriate response in your income statement, the monetary report that outlines every one of the business exercises, expenses of delivering or purchasing the items or administrations sold, and costs caused so as to maintain the business.

Income statements condense the money related exercises of a business during a specific bookkeeping period (which can be a month, quarter, year, or some other timeframe that bodes well for a business' needs).

Typical practice is to incorporate three bookkeeping periods on an income statement: the present time frame in addition to two earlier periods. So a month-to-month statement shows the present month in addition to the two earlier months; a quarterly statement shows the present quarter in addition to the two past quarters, and a yearly statement shows the present year in addition to the two earlier years. Giving this much data gives income statement business owners a perspective on the business' acquiring patterns.

The five key lines that make up an income statement are

Sales or Revenue: The aggregate sum of cash taken in from selling the business' items or administrations. You compute this sum by totaling every one of the deals or income accounts. The top line of the income statement will be either deals or incomes; either is alright.

Cost of Goods Sold: How much was spent so as to purchase or make the merchandise or administrations that were sold during the bookkeeping time frame in the survey. I tell you the best way to ascertain the cost of products sold in the area "Discovering Cost of Goods Sold."

Gross Profit: How much a business made before considering activities costs; determined by subtracting the Cost of Goods Sold from the Sales or Revenue.

Operating Expenses: How much was spent on working the business; qualifying costs incorporate regulatory charges, pay rates, publicizing, utilities, and different tasks costs You include every one of your costs accounts your income statement to get this aggregate.

Net Income or Loss: Whether or not the business made a benefit or shortfall during the bookkeeping time frame in the survey, determined by subtracting all-out costs from Gross Profit.

Organizing the Income Statement

Before you really make your business' income statement, you need to pick an organization in which to arrange your money related data. You have two choices to browse: the single-step position or the multi-step group. They contain similar data yet present it in somewhat various manners.

The single-step design bunches all information into two classifications: income and costs. The multi-step design isolates the income statement into a few areas and gives the businessman some key subtotals to make examining the information simpler.

The single-step design enables students to figure indistinguishable subtotals from show up in the multi-step group; however, those estimations mean more work for the business owners/readers. In this way, most organizations pick the multi-step configuration to simplify income statement investigation for their outside budgetary report business owners.

Setting up the Income Statement

Before you can set up your income statement, you need to figure Net Sales and Cost of Goods Sold utilizing data that shows up on your work-sheet, which I clarify in Chapter 16.

Discovering Net Sales

Net Sale is an aggregate of every one of your business less any limits. So as to figure Net Sales, you take a gander at the details with respect to deals, limits, and any business charges on your worksheet. For instance, assume that your work-sheet records Total Sales at $20,000 and $1,000 in limits given to clients. Likewise, as indicated by your worksheet, your business paid $125 in Credit Card Fees on deals. To locate your Net Sales, you subtract the limits and Visa expenses from your Total Sales sum, leaving you with $18,875.

Discovering Cost of Goods Sold

Cost of Goods Sold is the aggregate sum your organization spent to purchase or make the products or administrations that you sold. To ascertain this sum for an organization that purchases its completed items from another organization so as to offer them to clients, you start with the estimation of the organization's opening stock (that is the sum in the stock record toward the start of the recording period)

To disentangle the model for figuring Cost of Goods Sold, I've accepted the Opening (the estimation of the stock toward the start of the bookkeeping time frame) and Ending Inventory (the estimation of the stock toward the finish of the bookkeeping time frame) values are the equivalent. See Chapter 8 for insights regarding calculating stock worth. So to compute Cost of Goods Sold utilizing the detail on

Drawing remaining Sums from your Worksheet

After you compute Net Sales and Cost of Goods Sold (see the previous sections), you can utilize the remainder of the numbers from your worksheet to set up your business' income statement.

It's standard practice to show three bookkeeping periods on an income statement (see the area "What Is an Income Statement?"), so the accompanying model records three months of figures (however, just shows real numbers for one month).

Measuring your Cost of Goods Sold

Organizations that make their very own items instead of getting them for the future deal must track stock at three unique levels:

Raw materials: This detail incorporates the acquisition of all things used to make your organization's items. For instance, a fudge shop purchases every one of the fixings to make the fudge it sells, so the estimation of any stock available that hasn't been utilized to make fudge yet ought to show up in the detail of the crude material.

Work-in-process stock: This detail shows the estimation of any nudge that is being made; however, aren't yet prepared available to be purchased. It's impossible that a fudge shop would have anything in this detail, considering fudge doesn't take in excess of a couple of hours to make. Notwithstanding, many assembling companies take weeks or months to create items and hence, for the most part, have some segment of the stock an incentive in this detail.

Finished-products stock: This detail records the estimation of stock that is prepared available to be purchased. (For an organization that doesn't make its own nudge, completed merchandise stock is equivalent to the stock detail.)

On the off chance that you stay with the books and that fabricates its very own items, you can utilize a modernized bookkeeping framework to follow the different stock records portrayed here. Nonetheless, your fundamental bookkeeping framework programming won't cut it — you need a further developed bundle so as to follow various stock types. One such framework is the Premiere release from QuickBooks, which sells for around $500.

Unraveling Gross Profit

Entrepreneurs should cautiously watch their gross benefit inclines on the month-to-month income statements. Net benefit drifts that show up lower from one month to

The following can mean one of two things: Sales income is down, or Cost of Goods Sold is up.

On the off chance that income is down month-to-month, you may need to rapidly make sense of why and fix the issue so as to meet your business objectives for the year. Or then again, by looking at marketing projections for that month in earlier years, you may prevent mine that the drop is only a typical deal log jam since time is running short of a year and isn't cause to hit the frenzy button.

On the off chance that the descending pattern isn't ordinary, it might be an indication that a contender's successfully drawing clients from your business, or it might show that clients are disappointed with some part of the items or administrations you supply. Whatever the explanation, setting up a month to month income statement gives you the ammo you have to rapidly discover and fix an issue, in this way limiting any negative hit to your yearly benefits.

The other key component of Gross Profit and Costs of Goods Sold can likewise be a major factor in a descending benefit pattern. For instance, in the event that the sum you spend to buy items that you, at that point sell goes up, your Gross Profit goes down.

Checking Expenses

The Expenses segment of your income statement gives you a decent outline of all the cash you spent to keep your business working that wasn't legitimately identified with the clearance of an individual item or administration. For instance, organizations, for the most part, use publicizing both to acquire clients and with the expectations of selling a wide range of sorts of items. That is the reason you should list promoting as an Expense as opposed to a Cost of Goods Sold. All things considered, once in a while, would you be able to interface a promotion to the closeout of an individual item. The equivalent is valid for all the regulatory costs that go into maintaining a business, for example, lease, wages and pay rates, office costs, etc.

Entrepreneurs watch their cost patterns near be certain they don't crawl upwards and bring down the organizations' primary concerns. Any cost-cutting you can do on the cost side is ensured to expand your main concern benefit.

Utilizing the Income Statement to Make Business Decisions

Numerous entrepreneurs think that it's simpler to analyze their income statement patterns utilizing rates as opposed to the genuine numbers. Computing these rates is simple enough — you basically isolate each detail by Net Sales.

Testing Profits

With a finished income statement, you can do various speedy proportion trial of your business' benefit. You absolutely need to know how well your business made a contrast with other comparative organizations. You additionally need to have the option to check your arrival (which implies what rate you made) on your business.

Three regular tests are Return on Sales, Return on Assets, and Return on Equity. These proportions have considerably more significance on the off chance that you can discover industry midpoints for your specific sort of business, so you can look at your outcomes.

Profit for Sales

The Return on Sales (ROS) proportion reveals to you how proficiently your organization runs its tasks. Utilizing the data on your income statement, you can gauge how a lot of benefits your organization delivered per dollar of offers and how a lot of additional money you acquired per deal.

You compute ROS by separating total compensation before charges by deals. For instance, assume your organization had total compensation of $4,500 and offers of $18,875.

(On the off chance that your business isn't a partnership yet rather is controlled by a sole owner, you don't need to factor in any business charges in light of the fact that lone companies make good on income government expenses.

As should be obvious, your organization made 23.8 percent on every dollar of offers.

To decide if that sum calls for festivity, you have to discover the ROS proportions for comparative organizations.

Profit for Assets

The Return on Assets (ROA) proportion tests how well you're utilizing your company's advantages to create benefits. In the event that your organization's ROA is the equivalent or higher than other comparative organizations, you're working admirably of dealing with your advantages.

ROA can differ altogether, relying upon the kind of industry wherein you work. For instance, if your business expects you to keep up heaps of costly hardware, for example, an assembling firm, your ROA will be a lot of lower than a help business that doesn't require the same number of advantages. ROA can extend from beneath 5 percent for assembling organizations that require an enormous interest in apparatus and production lines to as high as 20 percent or much higher for administration organizations with not many resources.

Profit for Equity

To quantify how effective your organization was in winning cash for the proprietors or financial specialists, ascertain the Return on Equity (ROE) proportion. This proportion regularly looks superior to anything Return on Assets (see the former area) since ROE doesn't contemplate obligation.

Fanning Out with Income Statement Data

The income statement you produce for outside use — money related foundations and financial specialists — might be altogether different from the one you produce for in-house use by your chiefs. Most entrepreneurs like to give the base measure of detail important to fulfill outside clients of their fiscal reports, for example, outlines of costs rather than line-by-line cost subtleties, a net deals figure without revealing all the insight regarding limits and expenses, and an expense of merchandise number without announcing all the insight regarding how that was determined. The substance of the income statement is an altogether different story. With more detail, your administrators are better ready to settle on exact business choices. Most organizations create itemized reports dependent on the information gathered to build up the income statement. Things, for example, limits, returns, and recompenses, are generally hauled out of income statements and separated into further detail.

Discounts are decreases in the retail cost as a major aspect of an uncommon deal. They may likewise be as volume limits given to clients who purchase a lot of the organization's items. For instance, a store may offer a 10 percent markdown to clients who purchase at least 20 of a similar thing at once. So as to put their Net Sales numbers in context, entrepreneurs and directors must track the amount they decrease their incomes to pull in deals.

Returns are exchanges in which things are returned by the purchaser in any way, shape, or form — not the correct size, harmed, faulty, etc. On the off chance that an organization's number of profits increments significantly, a bigger issue might be the reason; in this way, entrepreneurs need to follow these numbers cautiously so as to recognize and resolve any issues with the things they sell.

Allowances spread blessings cards and different records that clients pay for forthright without taking any product. Remittances are really an obligation for business in light of the fact that the client (or the individual who was given the gift voucher) inevitably returns to receive stock and doesn't need to pay any trade out the return.

Another segment of the income statement that you're probably going to separate into more detail for inward use is the Cost of Goods Sold. Essentially, you take the detail gathered to ascertain that detail, including starting the stock, finishing stock, buys, and buy limits, and present it in a different report. (I disclose how to compute Cost of Goods Sold in the segment "Discovering Cost of Goods Sold" prior in this section.)

There's actually no restriction on the number of inside reports you can produce from the detail that goes into your income statement and other budget summaries. For instance, numerous organizations structure a report that takes a gander at month-to-month slants in income, cost of products sold, and income. Truth be told, you can set up your electronic bookkeeping framework (in the event that you utilize one) to consequently produce this report and other specially crafted reports.

Utilizing your mechanized framework, you can deliver these reports whenever during the month in the event that you need to perceive that you are so near gathering your month-end, quarter-end, or year-ultimate objective.

Numerous organizations will likewise structure a report that looks at genuine spending to the financial limit. In this report, every one of the income statement details shows up with their going with arranged spending figures and the real figures. In the event that you were exploring this report, you'd banner any detail that is impressively higher or lower than anticipated and afterward examine them to discover an explanation behind the distinction.

Chapter Thirteen

Preparing Books for a New Cycle

You will learn:

> *Closing the General Ledgers*
>
> *Analyzing the Customer Accounts*
>
> *Check for Unpaid Bills*
>
> *Move to a New Accounting Cycle*

In accounting, a bookkeeping period, or cycle, can be one month, a quarter, or a year (or other division of time in the event that it bodes well). At the end of each bookkeeping period, certain records should be shut while others stay open.

Similarly, as it's ideal for adding records to your accounting framework toward the start of a year (so you don't need to move data starting with one record then onto the next), it's ideal for holding up until the year's end to erase any records you never again need. With this methodology, you start every year crisp with just the records you have to best deal with your business' monetary exercises.

In this part, I clarify the records that must be shut and start with a zero balance in the following bookkeeping cycle (see Chapter 2 for more insight concerning the bookkeeping cycle, for example, incomes and expenses of merchandise sold. I additionally survey the records that proceed to start with one bookkeeping cycle then onto the next, for example, resources and liabilities. Moreover, I talk about the procedure of closing the books at year-end and how you start another bookkeeping cycle for the following year.

Settling the General Ledger

After you complete your bookkeeping work for the bookkeeping cycle in which your business works, it's an ideal opportunity to reevaluate your General Ledger. A few accounts in General Ledger should be focused out, so they start the new bookkeeping cycle with no detail from the past cycle, while different accounts keep on collecting points of interest starting with one cycle then onto the next. At the point when you separate General Ledger, the balance sheet accounts convey forward into the following bookkeeping cycle, and the income statement accounts start with a zero balance.

Focusing on Income Statement Accounts

At the point when you're certain that you've made every single required rectification and acclimations to your records and you have your cycle-end numbers, you can zero out all General Ledger accounts recorded on the income statement — that is incomes, Cost of Goods Sold, and business ledgers. Since the income statement mirrors the exercises of a bookkeeping period, these records consistently start with a zero balance toward the start of a bookkeeping cycle.

On the off chance that you utilize an automated bookkeeping framework, you may not really need to zero out the income statement accounts. For instance, QuickBooks changes your income and costs accounts at cycle-end to zero them out, so you start with a zero net gain; however, it keeps up the information in a document, so you're constantly ready to get to it. You can set your end date on the Company Preferences tab of the Preferences box (see Figure 22-1). To control who can make changes to earlier year accounts, you ought to likewise click Set Password (see Figure 22-2) to set an uncommon secret phrase for altering shut records.

Continuing Balance Sheet Accounts

Not at all like income statement accounts, you never zero out the records recorded on a balance sheet — that is, resources, liabilities, and value. Rather, you note your closure balances for every one of these records so you can set up a balance sheet (see Chapter 18), and you convey forward the information in the records into the following bookkeeping time frame. The balance sheet just gives you a depiction of the monetary condition of your organization, starting at a specific date in time. Starting with one bookkeeping cycle then onto the next, your advantages and (lamentably) liabilities remain, and you likewise need to keep up the data about how much value your financial specialists have placed into the organization.

Directing Special Year-End Bookkeeping Tasks

Before you start the way toward shutting the books for the year, print a synopsis of your record data from your modernized bookkeeping framework. On the off chance that you make a blunder while shutting the books, you can generally utilize this printout to backtrack and fix any issues.

QuickBooks gives a Year-End Guide Checklist (see Figure 22-3) to assist you with monitoring all the year-end exercises you have to do.

The agenda additionally incorporates connections to help screens that disclose how to do all the year-end shutting undertakings. You can scratch off each errand as you complete it and spare the registration to monitor your advancement during the end procedure.

After you complete all your year-end errands, you can gather and back up the entirety of your bookkeeping information for the year being shut. Most electronic recording frameworks have a procedure for consolidating and chronicling information.

Checking Client Accounts

As you set up your books for the finish of a bookkeeping cycle, survey your client accounts. Except if it's the year's end, you don't close the Accounts Receivable record, and when you start another bookkeeping cycle, you positively need to persist any balance still due from clients.

Before shutting your books toward the finish of the bookkeeping cycle, it's a smart thought to audit the client represents conceivable terrible obligation costs. Now's an ideal opportunity to be progressively basic of past due to records. You can utilize any awful obligation to diminish your duty nibble, so on the off chance that you accept that a client isn't probably going to follow through on a past due record, discount the misfortune.

Surveying Merchant Accounts

The finish of a bookkeeping period is the ideal time to audit your merchant records to be certain they're altogether come up with all required funds and prepared for the news cycle. Additionally, ensure that you've gone into your seller accounts any bills that reflect business movement in the period being shut; something else, costs from the period may not appear in the proper year-end fiscal summaries.

Survey any extraordinary buy requests to be certain that your merchant accounts aren't missing requests that have been finished yet not yet charged by the seller. For instance, in the event that you got stock on December 23, yet the seller won't charge for that stock until January, you should record the bill in December to mirror the receipt of that stock during that assessment year.

Erasing Accounts

The end procedure toward the finish of a bookkeeping year is a decent time to evaluate all your open records and check that regardless, you need them. In the event that a record has no exchanges in it, you're allowed to erase it whenever. Be that as it may, you should hold up until the year's end to erase any records that you don't think you'll require in the following year.

On the off chance that you utilize a mechanized bookkeeping framework, know that erasing a record erases every single past exchange in that record too. So on the off chance that you need to erase a record toward the year's end, you should stamp the record as latent rather with the goal that new exchanges can't be gone into the record accidentally.

Beginning the Cycle Anew

You positively would prefer not to close the entryways of your business as you set up the entirety of your year-end reports, for example, the fiscal summaries and legislative reports — all things considered, that can be a multi-month process. So you have to keep making passages for the New Year as you close the books for the previous year.

In the event that you do the books physically, you likely need simple access to two arrangements of books: the present year and the earlier year. In a manual accounting framework, you simply start new diary pages for every one of the dynamic records.

On the off chance that you have a few records that aren't extremely dynamic, as opposed to begin another page, you can leave some space for changes or adjustments, draw a line, and start the exchanges for the New Year in agreement.

In the event that you keep your books utilizing an automated bookkeeping framework, you can zero out the essential records to begin the New Year while leaving the information for the earlier year in the secret word ensured, shut records. You can, at present, make changes to those shut records, but are constrained to individuals who know the secret key — no doubt you, your bookkeeper, and your accounting supervisor.

Some portion of finishing off your books is beginning new petitions for every one of your records. Most organizations keep two years of information, the present year, and the earlier year, in the on-location office records, and put more seasoned documents into capacity. As you start another year, put away your two-year-old records for capacity and utilize the recently vacant drawers for the New Year's new documents. For instance, assume you're making documents for 2006. Keep the 2005 records effectively open in file organizer drawers in your office, however, put away the 2004 documents for capacity. At that point, keep your 2006 records in the drawers where the 2004 documents had been.

There's no immovable guideline about document stockpiling. You may find that you have to get to certain documents consistently, and along these lines would prefer not to place them in storage. Forget about it. Destroy out any documents identified with progressing movement and keep them in the workplace, so you don't need to rush to the capacity region each time you need the records. For instance, on the off chance that you have a progressing lawful case, you should keep any documents identified with that issue out of capacity and effectively available.

Chapter Fourteen

How to Manage your Cash with Books

You will learn:

Handle the Internal Bookkeeping

Monitoring Expenses and Profits

Dealing with Customers and Contractors in an Effective Manner

Any entrepreneurs consider accounting a bad thing, yet as a general rule, in the event that you utilize the information you gather, accounting can be your best mate with regards to dealing with your money. The way to exploiting what accounting brings to the table is understanding the estimation of essential accounting standards and utilizing data gathered. This section surveys the best ten different ways to utilize your books to assist you in dealing with your business money.

Graphing the Way

You may not feel that a rundown of records, called the Chart of Accounts, is worth a lot of consideration, yet this graph manages how you gather your money related information and wherein the books you put your organization's exchanges. With the goal for you to have the option to utilize the data viably, it's essential that your

Chart of Accounts characterizes each record correctly and decides precisely what kinds of exchanges go where.

Adjusting Your Entries

Balanced books are the best way to know how your business is getting along. Without them, you can never know whether your benefit numbers are exact. In accounting, you utilize a procedure called twofold section accounting to keep the books balanced.

Posting Your Transactions

So as to have the option to utilize the data you gather with respect to your business exchanges, the exchanges must be presented precisely on your records.

On the off chance that you neglected to present exchange on your books, your reports won't mirror that money-related action, and that is a major issue. Or on the other hand, on the off chance that you present an off base exchange on your books, any reports that draw on data will not be right — once more, an issue.

Following Customer Collections

On the off chance that your business offers to clients on store credit, you unquestionably need to be certain your clients pay for their buys later on. (Client account data is accumulated in the Accounts Receivable record just as in singular records for every client.) You should survey reports dependent on client installment history, called maturing reports, on a month-to-month premise to be certain clients pay on schedule. Keep in mind that you set the standards for store credit, so you might need to cut off clients from future buys if their records are past due for 90 days or more.

Taking Care of Tabs Accurately and On Time

In the event that you need to keep getting supplies, items, and administrations from your sellers and contractual workers, you should pay them precisely and on schedule.

Dealing with your installments through the Accounts Payable record guarantees exactness and practicality, and it additionally spares you from erroneously taking care of tabs twice. To be sheltered, you should audit maturing writes about your installment history to see that your accountant is making convenient and exact installments.

Arranging Profits

Nothing is more critical to an entrepreneur than the benefits he will ultimately make. However, numerous entrepreneurs don't set aside some effort to design their benefit desires toward the start of every year, so they have no real way to measure how well their organizations do consistently. Maintain a strategic distance from this issue by requiring some investment before the year begins to create benefit desires and spending that will assist you with meeting those desires. At that point, build up a progression of interior budgetary reports from the numbers in your accounting framework to help decide if you're meeting your business targets and keeping up authority over your item costs and working costs.

Contrasting Budget with Actual Expenses

Keeping a cautious watch on how well your spending arranging mirrors what's really occurring in your business can assist you with meeting your benefits objectives. Similarly, as with benefits (see the former segment), set aside some effort to build up spending that sets your desires for the year and afterward create inward reports that enable you to follow how intently your real costs coordinate that financial limit. In the event that you see any serious issues, right them at the earliest opportunity to be certain you meet your objective benefit toward the year's end. I talk progressively about interior money related detailing in Chapter 19.

Contrasting Sales Goals with Actual Sales

Notwithstanding watching your costs, you additionally need to screen your genuine deals, so they coordinate the business objectives you set toward the start of the year. Planning an inner report that tracks deals objectives versus real deals enables you to screen how well your business is getting along. On the off chance that you locate your genuine deals are beneath desires, right the issue as from the get-go in the year as conceivable so as to improve your odds of meeting those year-ultimate objectives. To discover how to utilize inward money related reports to follow your business action

Following Cost Trends

The consciousness of the costs associated with acquiring the items you sell or the crude materials you use to fabricate your items is significant on the grounds that these costs patterns can majorly affect whether your organization procures the overall gain you anticipate. On the off chance that you find that the expenses are inclining upward, you may need to change the costs of the items you sell so as to meet your benefits objectives. I talk increasingly about the following cost inclines in Chapters 8 and 19.

Settling on Pricing Decisions

Appropriately valuing your item can be a basic factor in deciding if your item sells. On the off chance that the cost is excessively high, you may not discover any customers ready to purchase the item; if it's excessively low, you lose cash.

While figuring out what cost to charge your clients, you should think about various components, including the amount you pay to purchase or manufacture the items you sell, statistical surveying about what clients will pay for an item, what you pay your workers, and promoting and administrative costs you bring about so as to set a cost. Every one of these things is factors in what you'll spend to sell that item.

Conclusion

Every business needs to incorporate accounting principles in their businesses. There are many accounting basics that are required by the businesses, and you need to make sure that the accountants in the company are well-versed with these principles. In this book, we have discussed all the accounting principles in detail and have highlighted the importance of these accounting principles in a proficient manner.

Keep these accounting principles in mind, and they will help you manage the business accounts and money in a business. The content presented in the book can be useful for both new and well-established businesses alike.

Made in the USA
Monee, IL
06 February 2020

21397559R10079